TODAY'S
PRINCE
TOMORROW'S
KING

DONETRUS G. HILL

TODAY'S
PRINCE
TOMORROW'S
KING

TATE PUBLISHING
AND **ENTERPRISES**, LLC

Published by Tate Publishing & Enterprises, LLC
127 E. Trade Center Terrace | Mustang, Oklahoma 73064 USA
1.888.361.9473 | www.tatepublishing.com

Tate Publishing is committed to excellence in the publishing industry. The company reflects the philosophy established by the founders, based on Psalm 68:11,
"The Lord gave the word and great was the company of those who published it."

Book design copyright © 2015 by Tate Publishing, LLC. All rights reserved.
Cover design by Ivan Charlem Igot
Interior design by Mary Jean Archival

Published in the United States of America

ISBN: 978-1-68028-564-2
1. Religion / Christian Life / Men's Issues
2. Self-Help / Spiritual
15.01.02

To you, because you are "today's prince, tomorrow's king"
I dedicate this volume to you!

PERSONALIZED MESSAGE

Prince Roman JaVaris Hill,

May your life bring forth the abundance of joy, love, and strength your name symbolizes. Son, you are tomorrow's king. Walk into your kingdom with humility and grace!

Refuse to live beneath your expectations!

Love,
Dad

CONTENTS

FOREWORD
BY JIM BERRY

Today's Prince, Tomorrow's King was introduced to me informally when Donetrus G. Hill preached at our church on Sunday, June 9, 2013. He quoted a small portion from the book, but he did not imply that he was the author. Instead, he stated, "This quote is from an unpublished manuscript." If you know Donetrus, then you know that this is his usual unpretentious manner.

I sat and pondered about what I was hearing. I thought, *What a deep, thought-provoking quote from an author I will never have the pleasure to meet or read.* Concluding our worship service, I was pleasantly surprised to find out that I indeed knew the author, and he gave me a copy of the manuscript. I read and read and continued to read.

The more I read, the more captivated I became with his authenticity and transparency. He speaks to the naiveté of young African American males and speaks from the vantage point of a seasoned African American male. He possesses the rare capacity to view the awkwardness of the past from his rearview mirror while experiencing the present and viewing the future simultaneously.

Donetrus, in this great work, marries two concepts, which in the twenty-first century, have long been divorced. He marries salvation (religion) and education; the child this union produced was an African American male who is well-balanced and ready for life as a productive citizen. I have often thought that education without salvation would produce deprivation. Donetrus has the uncanny ability to bring both education and salvation together, and his argument is very appealing, which seems to be the point the author makes. He earnestly desires for young men to examine their lives and take full responsibility for their decisions, realizing consequences are forthcoming.

Those who read this book will find it very engaging and thought-provoking. Donetrus speaks candidly to the *now* generation, and I believe he is on point because he speaks in a prophetic voice to the young African American male population. I am elated that my son has a copy as well. This book is a must-read.

—James "Jim" Berry, MDiv

FOREWORD
BY JAMES BOLTON, PHD

Nothing beautiful can ever be built without first being in pieces, and in his inaugural book, Donetrus G. Hill gleans from each piece of his life and personal experiences to address every African American young man. Speaking directly and transparently to the reader in *Today's Prince, Tomorrow's King*, Donetrus clearly articulates to princes that there is never a spot where God is not. Donetrus understands young men, and he pierces the façade that young men tend to hide behind. Immediately gripping, *Today's Prince, Tomorrow's King* encourages African American males by convincing them that they are more than who they are at their worst.

I have known Donetrus since 1996, both as a man and as a minister. He has always been honest and straightforward, and he conveys those qualities in *Today's Prince, Tomorrow's King*. He not only communicates to the reader from his life, but from the lives of others, including the resounding voices of African American history. The statements made in this peerless book about boys (princes) becoming men (kings) have been examined and are evident truths. This is not a normal book lacking research, but a masterpiece that is substantiated from factual literature, which answers the unique questions princes face while becoming kings.

Each chapter makes you more enthused about reading the next. Something in this book can relate to every young African American male (princes) because of the uncommon insight and integrity found in each page. A source of wholeness, every word seems like a beat of the heart because Donetrus touches all areas of manhood—even those that are most painful and ignored. I have read many books that have dually encouraged and confronted me, but *Today's Prince, Tomorrow's King* is loaded with defining moments, and I know many readers will agree. There is not an overuse of clichés but practical principles that keep changes from turning into crises in the lives of young men. Theologically sound, Donetrus even demonstrates how education and regeneration are necessary as a partnership, where God gets the glory, and the princes get the good.

Faith is your action toward what you desire, and every prince has certain stages and seasons they must progress through in order to become a king. *Today's Prince, Tomorrow's*

King presents guidelines for princes that are penetrating, pungent, and powerful. The method and the message of this book will advance the livelihood of every reader. So as you read this book, take notes and revisit those notes as needed. I highly recommend this book to every single mother raising a boy, any father nurturing a son, and all churches with male youth groups. This is a great book for those (princes) who are confused about their purpose, as it challenges the reader to investigate his existence.

Donetrus has written *Today's Prince, Tomorrow's King* from such a vantage point that it should be in every place (households, schools, athletic centers) that houses African American growing men. The book's cover will captivate you, but the content will change your calling and your character—forever.

—Dr. James J. Bolton
Author, molecular biologist, and minister

PREFACE

It was around 5:00 a.m. on what was supposed to be a normal Sunday morning. I had every intention of getting up and going to church as I've done countless Sundays prior to this one. On purpose, though, I was awakened by God to write words inspired by Him. I felt a stir in my spirit and in my mind that was quite unusual but very welcome. I could hear the chapters echoing in my ears and feel them in my heart. I knew it was imperative that I begin to write this book.

Today's Prince, Tomorrow's King is a necessary read for times such as these. Too often we read in the newspaper or watch on TV African American males being carted off in handcuffs, preparing themselves to serve an extended amount of time in prison for crimes that could have been avoided if only someone took the time to share with them that there is always an alternative. Or we see African American males involved in some heinous or unscrupulous act of organized criminal activity, such as selling or using drugs; robbing a neighborhood, institution, or business; or stealing vehicles. If only someone would have taken the time to inspire them through literacy and education, their outcome could have been different.

There are also the instances where African American males give up on their dreams and their families by dropping out of school, getting involved in gangs, or denying the children they produced—not to mention participating in incidents of random acts of violence and murder, reducing the number of viable young men poised to be the future leaders of this generation.

While these acts occur in every race and ethnicity, the intent of this book is to afford African American males, both young and old, the opportunity to embrace literature written specifically and purposefully for them. The intent of this book is to inspire and create opportunities that seem hidden or aloof, not only in our circumstances, but also in our mind. *Today's Prince, Tomorrow's King* is a necessary conversation for all who want a deeper understanding of the beauty and prowess associated with not only their birth, but also their legacy, which only they can leave. No one else can leave the impact or impression on society that you can!

African American males are becoming an endangered species in a population where they are continually being produced. See, conception and reproduction do not render strong, capable, confident men; they just increase the population and contribute to the census. I say that now is the time where black men and boys alike begin to reclaim their rightful place as leaders and not followers. The only way for that to occur is through family, commitment, and education.

African American males are experiencing both physical and emotional deaths. They are giving up on their dreams and aspirations due to meager beginnings, frustration, lack of education, lack of commitment, distrust, poverty, using illegal life-altering and physiologically destructive drugs, abandonment, and a lack or sense of belongingness necessary for every individual to feel safe and whole. We have a responsibility to address the issues and alter the trend. Spiritual acknowledgment and discipline, education, and family security are the only ways to break the curse. The time for change is now!

There is something special and precious inside each of us. The message of this book is to annotate the issues suffocating us as African Americans while also promoting the instances of success and triumph. We as a community need to rectify some problems and, on the other hand, take pride in and appreciate the sacrifices and commitments of those who left a legacy for us to emulate and complete. The moment for us to make a significant dent in history and leave a lasting impression on this world—to recognize that African American males are strong, capable, talented, honorable, successful, anointed, and determined individuals poised with the grace and the blessing of God—is nigh.

For too long, African American males have been considered inferior and inadequate, but now is the time for us to rise above our situations and disappointments and become the protectors of our families, the leaders of our organizations and corporations, and the heralded kings we were and are still created to be.

This book is spiritual because it unlocks the passion lying dormant inside African American males, which can only be summoned from the depths of our soul through struggle and attainment, harnessed by a power that only God can provide and create. This book is practical because we see an immediate need concerning the degradation of African American males targeted at diminishing and undermining the efforts, sacrifices, and contributions of our ancestors and living pioneers who felt the anointing to give their all so that this generation would have the ability to live with honor, self-respect, and dignity.

Though this book was created from several angles, the primary focus is to deposit hope and history so you will embrace the fact that you come from a people who gave tirelessly toward the reality you embrace today, and that it was vested and purchased with blood, sweat, and tears. This book is also poised to impress upon you that you have a responsibility to contribute merit and excellence toward the advancement of the next generation so it may continue to progress and prosper in all facets of life.

It is now time to embark upon this journey where you will recognize how capable and purposed you are to evolve and create change in your reality. As this journey begins, recognize that today, whether you know it or not, you have been identified as royalty. There is a crown and a throne with your name on it. Take ownership and great pride in knowing that in Africa, you were recognized with the distinction of being labeled a prince and eventually king. Today, the call to glory has returned! Though a prince today, you are tomorrow's king!

1

YOUR MAJESTY

*So God created man in his own image. And God
blessed them and said, "Have dominion over every
living thing that moves upon the earth."*

—Genesis 1:27–28

Prince Calvin

Almighty God, Creator of heaven and earth (Gen. 1:1),
decided to make a deposit into His new creation. Because
of His omnipotence, He was able to do the impossible. He
created life from the dust of the ground, and it goes without
saying that everything God made was "good." I submit to

you, my young brother, that you are the creation of God. And according to scripture, everything God made was good. You are no exception! Though your beginnings may not have been good, it has no bearing on your end. Yesterday may not have been a good day. Today may not be a good day, and truth be told, tomorrow may be worse than today, but I declare to you that as you begin to understand just how blessed and important your existence is to this world, you will understand that all you have been through was necessary to prepare you for what's to come.

SELF-IDENTIFICATION

Whether you know it or not, my brother, you are a *king*. You may look around and see poverty. You may look around and see turmoil and distress. You may look around and see a dismal, bleak future, but I submit to you this day that God has given you dominion and power to change what is to what it should be. God has given you dominion to change what has been embedded in your mind and transform your thinking. God has given you dominion to rise though you've always been made to feel beneath. God has given you dominion to speak in the midst of chaos, and all will listen. God has given you dominion to live out your greatest dreams and desires once you recognize the true majesty inside you. Young prince, God has anointed you to be a king.

DOMINION AND POWER

Now that I have your attention, let's look at the term *dominion*. Dominion is defined as having authority. Those who have dominion have the power to rule, the power to govern, and the power to change or transform situations and states of mind. According to scripture, God gave Adam dominion in the garden. In essence, God's greatest creation has the authority to name the unknown, to make declarations, and to set things in order. Despite what you think or have been told or made to believe, you have the same authority too!

To you, my brother, I submit that somewhere along the way, we have forgotten that God has given us this same power. Though it was a garden experience, I believe the spiritual implication is that man's dominion was supposed to grow and flourish in the days to come. As a man, it's paramount that you understand how important and necessary your position is in this world. Though young, now is the time to prepare your mind to be an aggressive learner, a hardworker, a protector, and a provider.

Now is the time that you, a young man, a prince, and a future king, operate within the parameters of impeccable character and the truest form of dominion. Not as a dictator, not as a tyrant, not as a bully, or an abuser of people and their feelings, but as a benevolent friend, a scholar, a leader, a conscious husband and father, and above all else, a God-fearing man. For God is love (1 John 4:8). And though you may not have seen the greatest examples of love, I welcome you to continue on this journey throughout this book to understand what it means to love unconditionally, to love blindly, and to love despite opposition and disappointment.

As a future king, it is important that you embrace these principles.

WHAT IS A KING?

I conducted several interviews with teenagers and young adults and asked, when they hear the word *king*, what does it mean to them? Though I received a plethora of answers, one consistent theme reigned supreme: power and money. Every young man whom I spoke to was concerned about power and money. Not one time did I hear that a king is a leader, a king is gracious, a king operates in integrity and honor. Nor did I hear that a king watches over his subjects.

Today, we associate power with money. We associate power with fancy houses and exotic automobiles. We associate power with expensive jewelry and name-brand clothes. We also associate power with the production of offspring and the abundance of sexual conquests. But, young prince, once you combine all these things, you realize just how little power you actually have. Yes, we all want to look nice, drive comfortably, experience lavish lifestyles, have pretty women in our arms, and eventually pass our genetic material on to the next generation, but the truest form of power or dominion is the realization that things will fade away, but your legacy and reputation will remain after the fame.

A king is responsible for those under his rule. A true king, in all of his royalty and majesty, realizes very quickly that he is no greater than the *least*. A king who understands his role in society and his kingdom embraces the burden of leadership while at the same time tasting the satisfaction of serving. Young man, if you don't get anything else out of this, I want you to understand that kings are not called; kings are born and eventually anointed.

YOUR DESTINY REVEALED

In 1 Samuel 10:1, it is recorded that the prophet Samuel took a vial of oil and anointed Saul to be the king of the Israelites. Make no mistake about it—Samuel received direct instruction from God to anoint Saul as king. It wasn't by chance. It wasn't because of popularity or by election. And it wasn't because of money. From his birth, though unaware, Saul was always the first king of the Israelites.

It doesn't matter how badly things look or how devastating and disappointing your situation is, greatness is and has been in you since the beginning. Let's look at another notable king—David.

In 1 Samuel 16:7, God sent Samuel yet again on a king-*identifying* mission. Notice I did not say a king-*finding* mission but rather a king-*identifying* mission, because if you recall, kings are chosen from birth. They are God-appointed and anointed. According to scripture, Samuel was told to visit the house of Jesse. God gave him strict instructions not to look at the exterior. He informed Samuel not to judge the young men based on either their height or their stature because God looks at the heart. Samuel, being obedient, studied the sons of Jesse and realized that none of the young men he viewed was "the intended."

In the eleventh verse of the same chapter, Samuel asked Jesse, "Are these all your children?" Jesse responded, "There is another, the youngest, but he keeps the sheep." Samuel instructed Jesse to send for him and said he would wait patiently. When David appeared in the twelfth verse, Samuel noticed that David was the very picture of health. He was bright-eyed and good-looking. It was at that moment when God instructed Samuel by saying, "Rise to your feet! Anoint him! He is the one!"

I could continue to introduce kings whose birthright gave them access to the crown, but what I want you to focus on now is the fact that both the kings mentioned above were kings before their awareness. Your Majesty, I humbly submit that you too are just as chosen to rule, reign, and affect the world with the crown you will eventually wear. See, you may have been told sometime in your life "You were a mistake," "You won't amount to anything," "I wish you were never born," "You're ugly," "You're stupid," "You won't graduate," "You have no purpose," "You have no place or position in this world"—but I have come to eradicate that false perception about your life.

Though a prince today, you are tomorrow's king! Your words have power. Your walk is full of authority. You are beautiful inside and out, and your existence matters. You may be angry, but God wants to give you peace. You may be tired, but God wants to give you rest. You may be hurting, but God wants to give you healing. You may have struggled through school, but God wants you to know that He created you, and that everything worth having is worth fighting for, worth struggling for, worth hurting for, worth sacrificing for, and, in some regards, worth dying for.

When I speak of dying, I am not indicating a physical death but rather a death to oneself where you identify issues and instances in your life that bring about corruption or destruction. All life is precious, and yours is no exception. Regardless of what you're involved in, kill the issue but preserve and embrace life.

It's time to elevate your thinking, young man! You are royalty! You are blessed! You are a child of the Most High! And because of your birth, because of your trials and tribulations, and because of your authority and dominion, you can speak to your situation and change it by declaring, "What once was will no longer be!"

There is an intrinsic power resting inside you, and now is the time for you to unleash your inner royalty. What you were told you couldn't have, I declare it's yours! What you were told you couldn't be, I declare it's so! What you were told you wouldn't amount to, I declare you are now a conqueror!

What you were told was not yours, I declare that, by faith, you have what you say you have! Young man, prince, future king, you are powerful. You are intelligent. You are creative. You are blessed. You are a survivor. And you are royalty!

Take the backseat no longer, for kings ride in the front. Slack in your classes no longer because kings are the heads of state. Remember, as a future king, you must speak with authority but make sure what you're saying is what needs to be said. Because of your strength and dominion, your words have power, and they must be used appropriately with consideration of others. For the scripture says, "God has not given us the spirit of fear; but of power, and of love, and of a sound mind" (2 Tim. 1:7).

Now that you realize how important you are and that inside *you* is a future king, let us begin this journey. American poet Don Williams Jr. said, "Our lessons come from the journey, not the destination."

2

THE WRONG "N" WORD

*I freed a thousand slaves; I could have freed a
thousand more if only they knew they were slaves.*

—Harriet Tubman, former slave and abolitionist

Prince Rhema

With today being such a technologically advanced age, we often lose sight of what's important. Majority of you who read this book probably don't know the joy associated with spending quality time with the elders embracing your family history. Because of the Internet, social media, twenty-four-hour television, and on-demand movies, the richness of conversations at the dinner table or family time uninterrupted by a text message or phone call is probably unrealized. Because of inflation and the need for parents to work day in and day out to support the family, young men like you are left to figure things out without proper guidance and directed inspiration. Though it's not your fault, if this trend does not change, inevitably, it will be your problem.

YOUR LEGACY

Family is important. In the African American community, family is the cornerstone of continuity and reconnection to what was and what is. Weddings, funerals, graduations, and family reunions provide us with organized gatherings essential to the remembrance of struggle paired with the notion of overcoming. It's an opportunity for you to connect and reconnect with your loved ones and embrace the traditions, experiences, and victories of the elders who paved the way for both you and me so we wouldn't have to suffer unnecessarily.

Unfortunately, this model, as with other mechanisms used to keep the family strong, has evolved over time, and as a result, traditions and history have been lost with every emerging generation. I will be honest with you: I'm trying to paint a picture before I dig into this chapter. My goal is a multipurpose one. I want you to think about your family in a manner reflective of what they have shown you and how much you've embraced from the lessons.

You see, African American males are not taking the time to recognize struggles and the accomplishments of their ancestors. They are taking their freedom for granted. My goal in this chapter is to figuratively hit you with a roundhouse kick to the neck followed by a quick jab to the throat. Not to be violent or malicious, but it's time for us to wake up and stop sleeping on the sacrifices of so many.

Too much blood has been shed for the freedom you now enjoy. Too much humiliation and embarrassment have been endured for the freedoms you now enjoy, and, future king, now that you recognize your royalty, it's time for you to embrace the sacrifices of your ancestors and acknowledge their contributions to the freedoms you now enjoy.

YOUR "ROOTS"

Make no mistake about it, regardless of what you read in your history books, what you see on television, and what you read on the Internet, your ancestors were slaves. They were brought here against their will. They were brought here forcefully. They were brought here with the purpose of never being returned to their families, friends, and loved ones. They were brought here to be servants. They were brought here to suffer. They were brought here to work. They were brought here to be broken. They were brought here to be weakened. They were brought here in chains. They were brought here in bondage. They were brought here to have no voice. They were brought here to serve a purpose with no compensation. They were brought here to create the American dream while living a complete nightmare.

Ultimately, after their purpose was served, they were brought here to die. They were abused, beaten, tortured, shackled, branded, raped, starved, humiliated, and disrespected, and they endured every other inhumane term associated with human suffering. They were exploited and stripped of their language, culture, traditions, and pride. Slavery was not a game. It was real. It happened. And what many of us are unaware of today is that it still exists. The only difference in the slavery of yesterday and the slavery of today is that *we* have the keys to take our own shackles off, but *we* refuse to do so.

As I indicated in the beginning of this chapter, my goal is to open your eyes to the atrocities and abuses endured by your own people. But I also want you to identify with the fact that you come from a lineage of survivors. Slave masters and overseers did any and everything they could to break the slave. Thankfully, they couldn't! Despite the hardships they endured at the hands of their oppressors, the slaves maintained a level of pride, dignity, and strength uncommon to many found in similar conditions. The owners did not take into account the spirit of the slave, the soul of the slave, and the strength of the slave. They did not consider the notion that there was an intrinsic motivation found deep within that would not allow the slaves to go down without a fight. The spirit of the slave would not allow them to give up on future generations. The spirit of the slave would not allow them to give up on you. Though they were being oppressed severely and violently, future king, you were on their mind. You were the reason they never gave up the fight for freedom and equality. See, your ancestors had a dream, and what many of us fail to realize is that we are living proof that the dream of the slave was not in vain.

The slaves endured hardship so you and I would have the opportunity to attend the best colleges and universities to be appropriately educated. The slaves endured hardship so you and I would have the opportunity to be CEOs, presidents, principals, and business owners. The slaves endured hardship so you and I would have the opportunity to hold our heads high and walk in dignity, honor, and self-respect. The slaves endured hardship so you and I would have the opportunity to stay connected as a family and never forget the traditions and customs of our ancestors while frequently telling the stories of perseverance and triumph.

Young brother, it is your purpose and responsibility to remember the blood, sweat, and tears shed by your ancestors as you progress in life, not to live in the past but to thrive in the future. Young brother, it is your purpose and responsibility to make sure you commit yourself to the betterment of your family and community by receiving a quality education, by exercising your right to vote, and by contributing to the legacy left by so many who have gone before you. Young brother, it is not for the next man to do, but rather, it's for you!

NIGGERS AND NIGGA—THE SAME DIFFERENCE

Now that you're all stirred up and you realize that, as a king, you have a responsibility to pay homage to those who have given themselves for you, there was one other thing of significance to our struggle today that was done to the slave and we shamefully continue: they renamed us and called us *niggers*. That's right, young men, once the slave was taken into captivity, he was no longer referred to as a king. He was no longer referred to as a prince. He was no longer referred to as a man. He and countless others were renamed and reclassified as *niggers*.

I realize that, for many of you, this is a shock because we continue the practice of disrespecting and denigrating ourselves by using the same terminology today.

By definition, a nigger is "someone who carries the plight and burden of slavery and racial discrimination, a person in oppression and ignorance. A nigger is someone who is lazy and unaware. A nigger is someone who is uncivilized, untamed, and unable to comprehend or learn. A nigger is barbaric and lacks sophistication and cannot adapt without force." My question to each of you reading this book is simple: Does the definition of a nigger adequately define you? Well—I'm listening!

If it doesn't, then why do we continue to subject ourselves to its disrespectful connotation?

I am a high school principal and hear these terms and phrases often: *nigga, niggas, my nigga, these niggas, them niggas, hoe-ass nigga, bitch-ass nigga,* etc. Young men—*enough!* It is shameful and degrading to the many who fought and died to come from under this depressing stigma. You're smarter than this. You have more education than this. You're more articulate than this. Elevate your conversation and speak with the eloquence and grace of a prince. When I come across this language, without hesitation, I address it. I ask the same question to whomever I'm speaking: "Why do you choose to disrespect not only this person, but also yourself by using such a negative term?" And without missing a beat, the respondent normally follows the path of so many others and says, "I'm not saying nigger. I'm saying nigga…there's a difference."

And my response is always the same: "No, sir, it's not."

See, there was a period of time when we had no choice as to what we were called. As African men and women brought to this country against our will, a nigger is what you were when you got on the boat. It's what you were while you endured the six- to ten-month ride in the belly of the boat. And when you finally hit land and realized that you were nowhere close to home, it's what you were as you adjusted your eyes to the dawning of a new period in your life.

Nigger is what you answered to and what you embraced to make sure you were not punished or even killed for being defiant and disrespectful. But today, we are so much more than what was forced upon us. Today, Your Majesty, you are a leader. You are educated, and you are FREE. So why choose to continue to use a term that associates you with bondage and slavery, knowing that you have access to more appropriate and eloquent titles?

You're a prince—a future king—and now is the time to embrace all the majesty and power associated with your position. Before we get too far ahead of ourselves, let's define what a *nigga* is. By definition, a *nigga* is a word evolved from the derogative term *nigger*. It has been categorized as a colloquial reference that black people can use toward other black people. It is synonymous with terms such as *homie*, *bro*, or *friend*. Young men, be not deceived. As indicated in the original definition, the word *nigga* is derived from the term *nigger*.

Make no mistake about it, whether you are called nigga by someone outside your race or foolishly say it to others, you are disrespecting the sacrifices and taking for granted the abuse suffered by slaves near and far. Whether your ancestors were slaves or endured the hardships of segregation dictated by Jim Crow laws, you should never embrace nor make allowances for the usage of such defiling vocabulary.

Nigger and *nigga* are pejoratives. A pejorative is a term of abuse meant to have derogatory intent. It is a word or grammatical form of expression that implies negativity and expresses contempt or distaste for another. If that's not you, young man, let it go!

THE PROPER "N" WORD—NOBLE

Though we have taken time to dredge up all the negative connotations associated with such a horrible span of time, we have reached the part where we can replace pejoratives used to keep us in shackles and bondage. It's time to lay aside everything in your life that is negative. It's time to lay aside everything in your life that will keep you bound. It's time to lay aside everything in your life that is mentally deflating, emotionally degrading, and spiritually invading to your newly discovered birthright.

As a prince, I don't want you to ever refer to yourself as or allow someone to call you a nigga. From this day forward, when you speak of yourself, when you speak of your brothers, I want you to embrace the term *noble*. See, in Africa, we were not savages as we were led to believe. We were kings and queens. In Africa, we were princes and princesses. We were considered royalty and embraced regal customs and traditions. To be noble means to have outstanding qualities. To be noble means that you are of a "high birth." To be noble means you are grand and impressive, especially in appearance. To be noble means you possess character, integrity, and honor. To be noble means you are characterized as being of superior mind and moral conviction.

These are terms that have not been associated with African Americans, but I want to encourage you today to realize that you are more than you thought you were. You are more than you were led to believe. You are more than what you see, hear, and feel. A noble gentleman recognizes and appreciates love, commitment, and sacrifice. A noble gentleman, which is what you are, is civilized and refined. He likes the finer things in life. He enjoys intellectual conversation and is not only a listener but also a contributor. Because you are noble, you are deemed aristocratic.

You are royalty. You are a prince. You are a future king. Choose your crown wisely and pick out a very plush throne because you are destined for greatness, and there is nothing that can stop destiny!

3

REAL MEN PRAY

And he spoke a parable unto them to this end that
men ought always to pray, and not faint.

—Luke 18:1

Prince Justin

Young man, I'm sure by now you have a deeper under-standing and appreciation for your significance and position in this world. You now know that you are reading a book written with the purpose of speaking into your heart, mind, soul, and situation to put you in a position to progress and advance yourself beyond the status quo.

LIKE A DIAMOND IN THE ROUGH

You're more than ordinary. You're more than typical. In fact, you're atypical, which means you're not common. You're not like your friends. You're not like your peers. You're not like anyone else in this world. You're unique. You're anointed. You're special, and in case no one ever tells you, you're a king with an awesome and bright future!

Now what do you think about that? See, from time to time, I feel the urge to remind you of how precious and rare you are. You're like a jewel, a diamond in the rough. A young man confident in his abilities while humble enough to receive instruction speaks volumes. We live in a time where everyone wants to speak but no one wants to listen. All have an opinion but never an explanation. Everyone has a problem, yet there are no solutions. But you are taking the steps necessary to position yourself in a manner where you recognize the need for assistance, guidance, direction, correction, and love. That, future king, and that alone, is the purpose of this book.

TO BE CHOSEN BY GOD

It's not easy being a man, but I tell you, it is definitely worth it.

God chose you! God chose you to lead. God chose you to protect. God chose you to provide. God chose you to love. God chose you. *God chose you.* Say it: "GOD CHOSE ME!"

Let's say that again: "God chose me to lead and not follow, to protect and not flee, to set the example and not make excuses, to love and not fight, to encourage and not hate, and to forgive and forgive and forgive again."

To forgive is oftentimes more difficult than the word implies. Forgiveness, though difficult at times, is the most powerful tool in your arsenal. To forgive takes you from being bound to having the ability to be free. To forgive unlocks the memories of past hurts and pains. To forgive is necessary for you to live.

Many people have hurt you, some unintentionally while others knew exactly what they were doing. But as a king, you owe it to yourself to forgive them so you can enjoy your latter days.

Take this time now and understand that to be chosen by God is also a declaration that you will choose to forgive and not begrudge.

There is a young man I know named Justin. He is currently a college student in Texas. He is continuing his education on a full academic scholarship because of his achievement in high school. He had his struggles, his setbacks, and his obstacles to overcome, but because he was determined, he made it! He and I were speaking one morning about the power of forgiveness. His exact words were, "I can't hold a grudge. I've had many reasons to be angry at people and cut them off, but it makes no sense. People make mistakes. We should forgive and keep forgiving until they get it right. Holding a grudge is stupid. It takes more effort to hold a grudge than to forgive them and move on."

These are words from an eighteen-year-old. Justin has seen his fair share of disappointment and frustration yet has taken the perspective not embraced by many, not even adults! Forgiveness is Jesus's commandment. Forgiveness *in* love is what Jesus expects from us.

First Peter 4:8(b) reads: "For love shall cover a multitude of sins." Jesus forgave in the face of tyranny, persecution, and execution. If He forgave and had no sin, why do we hold on to yesterday's anguish and hurt today? Your Majesty—let it go!

I know it hurts, and I know it was wrong, but forgive the perpetrator who abused you, misused you, mistreated you, abandoned you, and took your innocence from you. It wasn't your fault how you were harmed, but it is up to you to turn your misery into a miracle and turn your pain into progress.

Forgive them and advance your life without the stress of your yesterday. You are worth a fresh start. No one ever said that being chosen by God was easy, but I want you to embrace and recognize that it's a great feeling to be *chosen* by God!

Now, let's stop for a second. Because this is such a critical time in this section of the book, some of you reading may want assistance with asking God to forgive those who have spitefully used and mistreated you. If that's you, say this prayer with me with passion and sincerity. Speak from your heart and personalize it any time you feel the need:

Father,

I recognize that I am not perfect and am in need of forgiveness too. I don't desire to continue to walk in shame about events that took place in my past. Please, Father, forgive me for my sins and transgressions as I forgive those who have sinned against me. I'm tired of reliving the agony. I'm tired of enduring the stress and shame. I am asking You this day to forgive those who attempted to destroy my spirit, destroy my love, and destroy my innocence. I forgive them, God, and I pray that You release me from my past so that I may move forward in love and peace. Touch my life, God, and make it new. Touch my heart, God, that I may love again. Touch my mind, God, that I may trust and believe in those who have let me down time and time again. Thank You, God, for bringing forgiveness into my heart, and I ask now that You anoint me to embrace my former enemies in love and respect. Thank You for delivering me from my past. In Jesus's name, I seal my forgiveness with His blood.

Amen.

Whoever knew that being a man, even a young man, came with so much responsibility and dedication? I'm sure that after reading the first two chapters, your eyes are now opened to the power and dominion resting inside you while also illuminating the possibilities of you establishing a kingdom on earth in which you embrace your subjects; educate yourself thoroughly; support your family and friends; walk with honor, integrity, and nobility; and embody a sense of self-respect and dignity uncommon to most. Future king, if you realized all these things up to this point, then keep reading because you are well on your way to a more fulfilled, purposeful life. While we have addressed so many characteristics and traits that princes and future kings personify, it is imperative that royalty establish and maintain a communicative relationship with God the Father.

For without seeking His guidance and direction for your life, all that is and all that will be are lost.

WHO IS GOD?

Recently I was blessed with the opportunity to teach a class on prayer at a youth conference. My purpose was to speak to two different age groups about the significance, the necessity, and the act of praying. In essence, my mission was to teach children and young adults why they need to pray and how to do it.

By now, I'm sure you recognize that I am very passionate about what I believe, and in teaching at the youth conference, I made sure that my attendees felt as strongly about praying as I did.

The previous statement was to let you know that when you really believe something, it's okay to articulate and express yourself while maintaining dignity and decorum. No *ratchetness*!

Make no mistake about it, I love God! God is the best thing that ever happened to me. A relationship with Him has allowed me to maneuver through some of the most difficult times in my life.

In 2002, I unexpectedly lost my brother. He died in his sleep from heart failure. He was living a normal life, very active and engaging. One evening, though, God saw fit to call him home. He was twenty-one years old, leaving me with only the memory of my younger sibling, my best friend. And yes, make no mistake about it, that was the most difficult season of my life. I had never experienced pain like that before. I cried, "But God!" God embraced my heart and enveloped me in a cradle of support and transition. I say again, "But God!" God allowed me to continue in this life and harness strength that can only be produced through significant trial. Again I say, "But God!"

WHEN DO I PRAY?

I talk to God often. I read His Bible often. I pray to God in the car, in the shower, at work, at the grocery store, and anywhere else I choose. See, God is not as formal as we have been made to believe. There is no requirement that says you have to abase yourself physically every time you talk to God, though humbling yourself is a requirement. All He wants is to be glorified and spoken to about what's real in your life.

How Do I Pray?

God expects you to be honest and sincere when you speak to Him, not arrogant and cocky. He knows what you're going to say before you say it, but you still need to say it. God is bigger than any of your problems, but He will get involved only when you invite Him in. Lower yourself so He can elevate you. Talk to Him often so He can heal your pain and forgive your mistakes. Allow yourself to be transparent and "be real" when you talk to Him. God sees and hears everything. It's okay to tell Him all about what you've done and why you did it. Respect His royalty, and He will establish yours!

Here is an example of a simple prayer I just prayed about this book:

> Father,
>
> I pray that You bless this book and all those who read it, that they might be blessed and believe in their abilities. In Jesus's name, amen!

Let's say I need to say a prayer of repentance because I lied to my mother about where I was last night (this really happened when I was your age!):

> God,
>
> Please forgive me for lying to my mother. I know what I did was wrong, and I thank You for keeping me safe. I recognize that I am a liar and I need Your help so

that I can change my ways. Please, God, forgive me for lying to my mother. I am going to work very hard in making sure I don't do that again. My mother has been good to me, and she doesn't deserve to be lied to. I apologize and repent to You, and I pray that she can forgive me as well. In Jesus's, name I pray. Amen.

Again, these are examples of praying to God with a sincere heart. Once you ask God to forgive you, He will, but the premise behind it all is that you stop the behavior. Talk to God about all you do, both good and bad, and He will help you make better decisions. He is the best thing for your life!

JESUS—THE WAY, THE TRUTH, AND THE LIFE

I try to have as open a relationship with Him as humanly possible. I trust Him with my life because He created me. I trust Him with my problems because who better to fix me than *the One* who made me?

I believe in His power. I believe in His sovereignty. And I believe in His Son, Jesus the Christ, the Anointed One, the Redeemer, the Messiah, and my Savior!

I took time to list the attributes and characteristics of God and His Son, Jesus, because He has been that good to me, and I owe Him significant praise. See, my brother, oftentimes we are taught that "it doesn't take all that." But I want you to understand that according to John 3:16, "God so loved the world that He gave His only begotten Son that whosoever believeth on Him should not perish, but have everlasting life."

Not only does it take that but much more. God gave everything He had to make sure you and I could continue an active fellowship and relationship with Him.

Are you perfect? No! Does God still love you? Yes!

But I have messed up so many times. Will God forgive me? Yes!

I listed only a few questions and answers because those are the main things people want to know.

Does God love me? Will God forgive me? And even though I messed up, will He still choose to love me and use me? My brother, you need God in your life, and God is waiting for you.

But I'm sure your question to me is, Well, how do I get to know God in a personal and more meaningful way? I'm glad you asked!

KNOWING GOD

Getting to know God and having a relationship with Him isn't any different from introducing yourself to a classmate, a girlfriend, or even a stranger. It's all about making yourself available and having the desire to get to know them better. What you have to know is that God already knows everything about you.

God told Jeremiah the prophet, "Before I formed thee in the belly I knew thee, and before you came forth out the womb, I sanctified thee" (Jer. 1:5).

The same truth is applied to your life. God is not a stranger to you, neither you to Him. God desires for you to spend time talking with Him, reading His word, and asking questions that will cultivate a deeper understanding as to your purpose and destiny.

Many people who know God based only on what other people tell them have misconstrued perceptions and false realities as to who God really is.

God is love. God is gracious. God is giving. God is forgiving. God is good. As we already highlighted, God made a choice to sacrifice His Son for the sons and daughters of the world. He did so because he desired a relationship with His people. Because God is the ultimate King and there are no kings before Him, He has given us a practical example as to how you, a future king, should treat your subjects: always put the needs and feelings of others before yours.

God desires the opportunity to talk with you. This is the reason why men have to pray.

THE MODEL PRAYER

Prayer is the only way to communicate with God. In Luke 11:1–13, Jesus was praying, and when He finished, one of His disciples asked Him to teach them how to pray. Jesus, being the teacher and leader He was, taught them to pray. He made sure that they acknowledged God as the Father. He acknowledged the fact that sin was present and that they should ask God to forgive them for their sins. He made sure they knew that their needs would be met from His supply and that they must request what they needed each day from their Benevolent Father. He made sure they understood that temptation was real and that they needed God to lead them away from the path of unrighteousness. Jesus acknowledged that evil was present but reaffirmed the power of the kingdom. And at the end of the prayer, He told them to close it out with a term that means "the truth." He told them to finish with a term that means "I believe what I'm saying and I trust in my heart that it will be done." He told the disciples to close out every prayer with *amen*. Now, when we end prayers, we follow the same premise as the disciples were taught, but we include "In Jesus's name, amen!" Jesus told the disciples in John 14:14, "If you ask anything in My name, I will do it."

Young man, what I just provided you is a rubric for prayer. But make no mistake about it, prayer can be as simple as "God, I'm sorry," "God, I need you," God, thank you!" These are prayers. Though not formal and drawn out, they are very effective in reaching God and letting Him know how much you appreciate Him or need Him at any given time.

See, God is not as complicated as we make Him out to be. God just wants to know that you need Him, you appreciate Him, you love Him, and you desire to get to know Him better. To talk to God does not require a lot of thought. To talk to God does not require sophistication and fancy words. To talk to God, you don't need to be grammatically correct. To talk to God, all you need is a willing heart and an open spirit.

THE PROMISE TO A PRAYING MAN

The Bible says in 1 Thessalonians 5:17, "Pray without ceasing." You should pray all the time. As a young man, with all the temptations and stresses complicating your existence, a relationship with God through His Son, Jesus, will make the difference in your life. With so many temptations and distractions waiting for you, a relationship with God is the only thing that will keep you safe.

This generation, your generation, has to overcome obstacles and temptations including pride, envy, technology, sexual immorality, homosexuality, premarital sex, STDs, pregnancy, gangs, drugs, alcohol, peer pressure, bullying, low self-esteem, poverty, failure, neglect, abuse, suicide, and a host of other things that could very easily deter you from reaching your goals. Getting to know God intimately by reading His Word and having very open and honest conversations with Him could ultimately save your life and your future.

Am I telling you that in this world you will not experience trials, disappointments, setbacks, and frustrations? No. But I am telling you that an authentic relationship with God centered on trust and transparency will leave you more fulfilled and empowered to overcome every situation.

In this world, you will experience pain, but in God, you will experience relief. In this world, you will experience disappointment, but in God, you will experience encouragement. In this world, you may be used, abused, and mistreated, but in God, you will be blessed and highly favored. In this world, you may be rejected, ridiculed, and talked about, but in God, you will be elevated and restored to a higher weight in glory. Jesus is quoted in the scriptures as saying, "With men, it is impossible, but not with God; for with God, all things are possible" (Mark 10:27).

All it requires to have everything we have spoken about is faith. Faith in God and an appetite and interest to know more about Him will bless your life, for it is recorded in scripture, "He is a rewarder of them that diligently seek him" (Heb. 11:6).

THE FACTS

Future king, for all that we have shared, this is by far the most important section of this book. We have spoken about prayer and having a more personal, intimate relationship with God the Father. And though God has been interpreted many different ways, there is one link to the Father that cannot be ignored, and that is a relationship and acceptance of Jesus the Christ.

Jesus is God's only begotten Son. Jesus was born unto the Virgin Mary. His conception was enacted by the Holy Spirit. He walked the earth for thirty-three years and performed miracles and showed the greatest examples of love, affection, forgiveness, and sacrifice. He was crucified for the sins of the world. He hung, bled, and died, and was placed in a tomb;

three days later, He rose with all the power, majesty, dominion, and authority.

He was resurrected, and now sits at the right hand of the Father. John 3:17 says, "God did not send His Son into the world to condemn the world; but that the world through Him might be saved." According to John 14:6, Jesus says, "No man comes to the Father, except by Me."

THE INVITATION

During this time, today's prince, tomorrow's king, I implore you to seek God while He is near; and in your heart, through faith, acknowledge what is truth and recognize your need for Jesus in your life.

Jesus is God's Son. God sent Him to die in your place. All He requires from each of us is that we accept Him, love Him, and love our neighbors. To gain all that God has for you, acceptance of the Son is necessary to embrace the Father.

Salvation is a gift, but as with anything, the choice is yours. As Romans 10:9 reads, "If you will confess with your mouth that Jesus is Lord and believe in your heart that God raised Him from the dead, you will be saved." Jesus said in Revelations 3:20 said, "Behold, I stand at the door, and knock: if any man hears My voice, and opens the door, I will come in to him, and will eat with him, and he with Me." Jesus is indicating that He desires a relationship with you, but because He is a gentleman, He will wait until He is invited in.

If you don't already feel His presence, keep reading. In a few more sentences, you will begin to feel Him knocking!

Future king, make no mistake about it, "all have sinned and come short of the Glory of God" (Rom. 3:23). There is no escaping it. We have all messed up. We have all sinned. And we have all transgressed against God. The Bible records in Romans 6:23 that "the wages of sin is death; but the gift of God is eternal life through Jesus Christ our Lord."

As you can see, God has made provision for you and me to fellowship and have a communicative relationship with Him, but if you do not know Jesus in the pardon of your sins or have never asked Him into your life and accepted Him as God's Son and your personal Lord and Savior, you are missing the link that will give you salvation and forgiveness.

If that's you, here is your opportunity to secure atonement and everlasting life. Salvation and acceptance of Jesus requires faith. It requires you to believe in what you can't see but you know in your heart is real. I believe by faith that as you read this, you are beginning to sense God's presence in the room and that you feel something inside starting to "stir." That's the Holy Spirit, indicating that Jesus is standing at the door of your heart, knocking. He is waiting on you and desires to make you one of His own.

Do not let this opportunity pass you by because tomorrow is not promised. Accept Jesus today. If this is you, say the following with faith, honesty, sincerity, and love:

God,

I am a sinner seeking salvation. I recognize that You are real, and I need You in my life now and from this day forward. Please forgive me for my sins. Cleanse my heart and my mind that I may serve you. I accept Jesus the Christ, Your only Begotten Son, as my Lord and Savior. I believe He came to this world to die in my place, and I acknowledge that You raised Him from the dead. I believe in my heart that He is alive and well and sitting at Your right hand. I accept His sacrifice for my life and receive Him in my heart as my personal Lord and Savior. Please, God, save me from myself and anoint me to live for You. Allow Your Holy Spirit to come alive within me that I may receive comfort and power. In Jesus's name, I pray, thanking You for the gift of salvation and eternal life.

Amen!

Future king, if you prayed that prayer and believed it in your heart, by faith, I believe that you are now saved by grace, and everlasting life is yours. Now you must live an acceptable life by reading your Bible, praying to God through Jesus, and asking God to forgive you and cleanse you from all unrighteousness while also forgiving others for their malicious acts in your life. I encourage you to find a church that will assist you in your new walk with Christ and offer you comfort and guidance in knowing that you will mess up, but God's love and forgiveness endures forever.

God bless each of you, and welcome to the royal family. Remember, real men pray!

4

EDUCATION IS EVERYTHING

The function of education is to teach one to think intensively and to think critically. Intelligence plus character—that is the goal of true education.

—Rev. Dr. Martin Luther King Jr.

For every one of us that succeeds, it's because there's somebody there to show you the way out. The light doesn't always necessarily have to be in your family; for me it was teachers and school.

—Oprah Winfrey

Prince Jordan

Young man, by now I am certain that you understand your value and significance in this world. We need you! Your birth and your existence on this planet are not by accident. There is so much inside you. Because you are royalty, many will try to detract from your majesty.

Truth be told, if we had the opportunity, we would change some things about ourselves and our lives. Some would change their parents. Some would change their living conditions. Some would change their appearance and physical stature while others would change their future. But I encourage you, future king, to embrace everything about you and enhance it and morph it into the outcome you desire for yourself.

At no time should you desire to change your parents, for if you could, you would not be influenced by this book but rather someone else. If you desire a change in your living conditions, then I suggest you work hard, set goals, write a plan, and attack the plan until you accomplish what you set out to accomplish. The choice is yours. If you don't like your physical appearance and you feel like you need to work on your body and enhance muscle tone and lose a few pounds to better accentuate your inner beauty to match your outward expression of strength and power, then discipline yourself by eating healthy, exercising, and taking care of yourself by getting the necessary sleep and rest your body requires and not polluting your body with carcinogens and toxins found in processed foods or fast-food franchises.

Future king, with all your nobility, you have to do more than look and act like a prince or future king, you have to sound like a king. The only way to do that is to enhance and elevate your vocabulary and manner of speaking. This brings us to the focus of this chapter: *education*. Young man, you have a responsibility to educate yourself so that you can in turn contribute meaningful factual commentary and expertise to a generation starving for enlightenment and heightened awareness. It is not only your responsibility; it is your opportunity.

THE NECESSITY OF EDUCATION

I can remember being a child and vividly hearing my mother say, "You're going to college. Both you and your brother are going to get an education. And after you finish college, you're going to graduate school." My first memories of these directives came around the age of seven or eight. I can't tell you I always enjoyed school, but I will tell you I understood its value. I can't tell you I always wanted to go to school, but I will tell you I understood its value. I can't tell you I always saw myself graduating from high school, much less going on to college and then eventually graduate school to pursue higher education, but I will tell you that as I look back on my educational journey, it was well worth it. And to this day, it is still benefiting my life; in essence, I understand its value!

Future king, education is not an option. There is no excuse to give up on yourself by dropping out or quitting on such an attainable goal. An education is available for every person who desires one. Now, I will admit that every school does not have the student in mind. There are some pretty horrible schools. You may have the misfortune of sitting in a classroom where you have a tired, frustrated teacher. But I promise you that once you take ownership of your own academic success and future, you will begin to learn despite the teacher, despite the school, despite your past, despite the negative comments, and despite the frustration. The thing about receiving an education is that at the end of the day, it's *yours*. Your mind is capable of interpreting and retaining everything you desire to learn.

There's a maxim that says "the world is your oyster," which means you can sample and partake and learn from any culture, tradition, and subject you desire. The choice is yours. If you want a bare-minimum education, the choice is yours. If you want a decent education, the choice is yours. If you desire to ascend to the highest heights of academic prowess and achieve the ultimate in academic success, then, my brother, spread your wings and fly and let nothing deter, distract, or discourage you from reaching the academic pinnacle you desire to achieve. Remember, the choice is yours!

YOUR POSITION AT SCHOOL

I graduated from CE Byrd High School in Shreveport, Louisiana. I graduated in the top 25 percent of the class with a solid B-grade point average. I also graduated from the math-science magnet program, which operated as a "school within a school." What that means is several students applied and were selected to interview for the magnet program and could attend the school regardless where they lived. Many of us were African American students who were attracted to the school because of the opportunities a prominent school like Byrd represented, which could not be found in the schools in our neighborhoods.

Though Shreveport is an urban city, my high school could be considered suburban though it attracted students from urban settings. I will admit I was not the best student. I struggled in high school, but I had some good teachers. One teacher who really sticks out in my mind and has always been coined as a favorite teacher was my eleventh-grade English teacher Ms. Evelyn Cox. Ms. Cox was an African American teacher who required me and the rest of my classmates to be the best at all times.

I was that student who would always try to be funny at the most inappropriate time. Ms. Cox made sure I understood that as a young black male in a school with such high Caucasian attendees, I needed to assert and insert myself as someone who should always be taken seriously and not give anyone the opportunity to make jokes at my expense though they appeared to be laughing with me.

What am I saying? As a student, your only priority and purpose is to learn. Not to make the class laugh, not to take away from the richness of the lesson, not to distract other students from learning because you're frustrated at what you didn't or don't understand, not to disrespect or defile the integrity and sincerity of someone trying to expand and broaden your horizons by adding to the body of knowledge you've amassed over the years. We have to stop taking our education for granted.

Both my mother and father supported me through education. They believed that without it, the alternative was not worth discussing.

DELAYED, NOT DENIED

As previously stated, I was not the strongest student. I did just enough to keep my grades somewhat competitive, knowing that I could have done more to be closer to the top of the class, if not at the top, but I chose to be more social and spent my evenings engaged in other activities rather than doing homework and studying to enhance what I learned during the day and cement it more into my long-term memory.

I was a crammer. I studied the night before the exam, would make a B, and would then be content. That's how I operated and saw no reason to do anything differently, but all that changed during my sophomore year. Our class was invited to attend the National Honor Society Induction Ceremony.

I sat in the audience and watched my friends, my peers, and my laughing buddies receive the certificate and NHS pin recognizing their academic efforts and accomplishments while I was sitting, not on stage but in the audience with everyone else who had not risen to the challenge of being a committed student.

See, future king, it's not enough to come to school; you have to be actively engaged in the learning process and participate in class while being involved in the lesson. That is the only way to extract what you need and contribute where you can. It is only at that point where true learning takes place.

I knew I should have been on stage with my friends, but because I felt like it wasn't that big of a deal, I was placed on the outside looking in. It was at that moment when I made a change to my academic priorities. I came home that afternoon, and I told my mother how badly I wanted to be in the National Honor Society. I can't recall what her response was, but I do know that every time I brought a C home, she would remind me. "I don't know how you expect to get in the National Honor Society bringing home grades like this." Now, on a sidenote, I am sure that in my mind, I had something *smart* or *clever* to say like, "What kind of grades did you bring home? Or where is your honor society membership card?" But, future king, unlike this generation, my generation had enough sense to only think such retorts but never say them audibly for fear that we would be, and I quote, "knocked into the middle of next week!" You are a future king and must always revere and respect your parents and any adult who deserves treatment as a parent. Okay, back to the story!

I struggled to make better grades, but I was consistent, dedicated, and determined to find a way to make it into the honor society. I had found I needed to work harder to make the grades that would raise my GPA so that I could be inducted into this elite organization. It wasn't easy, but it was definitely worth it.

I set a goal for myself, and I diligently worked at it for the next three semesters. I was entering my last semester of my senior year, and the opportunity to be inducted was fading away; but in April, I received a letter, unaware of its contents. I had no idea what the document stated, but as I opened it, I saw the seal of the National Honor Society. It confirmed my invitation to be inducted at the end of the month. I was so excited. Joy exuded from every pore of my body. I couldn't wait to get home to tell my mother about my accomplishment.

A goal that I had set some two years prior had finally become a reality. Future king, what I want you to take from this story is that when you set goals and work toward them, never wavering, never giving up, the goal or the blessing may be delayed, but it doesn't mean it's been denied.

I recall walking across the stage to receive my certificate, my National Honor Society pin, and the National Honor Society stole that I had the privilege of wearing for graduation three weeks later. I worked at it. I never gave up, and to God be the glory, I was inducted. And to you, I say, no matter where you are in your academic pursuits, keep working at being the best student possible, for the alternative is not worth discussing.

HISTORICALLY BLACK COLLEGES AND UNIVERSITIES (HBCUS)

It was the summer of 1996. To reiterate, I reached my goal of making the National Honor Society and finally culminated thirteen years of required studies by graduating from high school. At this point, my sights were set on college. I couldn't wait. I had received scholarships to a few big schools, but I made the decision to attend a small HBCU in Texas.

HBCUs serve a tremendous purpose in the African American community. There are more than one hundred HBCUs operating with the distinction of enduring the tests of time. HBCUs were created prior to 1964 with the intent of educating black students during an oppressed time. Most HBCUs were founded after the Civil War in southern states to increase the opportunities for freed slaves and their future generations to be educated.

Today, HBCUs provide students of all races and ethnicities the privilege of being educated without prejudice or persecution. HBCUs offer students the chance to embrace culture, tradition, and legacy.

They are inundated with the world's best and brightest. They have all the advancements and allowances of bigger, more "affluent" colleges. They range from two- to four-year universities and confer graduate degrees including medicine, law, and pharmacy.

HBCU students experience innovative learning opportunities while enjoying the rich culture, history, and tradition associated with being on the "yard." The athletics and social aspects are second to none, and a level of "soul" is found at HBCUs, which other colleges may emulate but never duplicate!

HBCUs are the cornerstones of our communities and need to be respected as the institutions that gave us a chance to have our spot at the table and be heard. As stated by Langston Hughes in his poem "I, too, Sing America"— "besides, they'll see how beautiful I am and be ashamed." For so long, because of misconceptions and preconceived notions, African Americans have not been valued or deemed influential or even relevant toward the advancement of innovation and achievement. Because of HBCUs, your voice will be heard because you speak with the passion and creativity of someone purposed and intelligent.

Though fine institutions of learning exist all over the world, the education and experience found in an HBCU is like no other. There is a sense of belonging attached to the whispers of ancestors who endured hardship for the opportunity you and I embrace to be educated at some of the nation's finest, most prominent, colleges, and universities.

HBCUs are still needed today as a reminder of where we've been and, ultimately, where we are going. I attended an HBCU and am thankful for the experience.

WILEY COLLEGE—A BEACON LIGHT

I attended Wiley College in Marshall, Texas. I made the decision to attend Wiley because it was attempting to resurrect its music program and offered me a full scholarship to be involved in the campaign. I will admit, in the beginning, I was not very impressed with the aesthetics of the college, but I was excited about the opportunities and experiences that lay ahead.

Wiley College was founded in 1873 by the Freedmen's Aid Society. Wiley's purpose was to educate newly freed slaves in the Jim Crow South and create opportunities for them in a system that did not fully recognize African American creativity and intellectual ability.

Wiley, like other HBCUs, was key to the advancement of African Americans in a time where archaic ideas still ran rampant on the "place" of the Negro. Segregation, racism, psychological and physical torture, and lynching were common practices in the rural South, but the young men and women of Wiley College were determined to be educated in the face of oppression and persecution.

The more I learned about my college, the more intrigued and excited I was about being there. As many of you now know, Wiley College is the home of the first black debate team allowed to compete against white debate teams, and to everyone's surprise except for those on the campus of Wiley College, they were not only competitive, they were also victorious.

So victorious that in 1935, they beat the national champions; and though they were never officially given the title, they earned it.

COLLEGE DAYS, IMBUED WITH MEMORIES FOND!

Wiley College is my alma mater. It became my home away from home. It is the place where I received my bachelor of science degree in biology. Wiley College is the place where I learned to articulate my ideas in a logical, coherent, and lucid manner while simultaneously being open to different perspectives and vantage points. Wiley College is the place where I learned how to struggle yet succeed, to embrace new ideas yet keep my convictions consistent, and to rely on myself as an individual yet contribute to the overall success of my brothers and sisters regardless of their backgrounds, opinions, or preferences.

The thing about college is that it teaches us who we are while embracing the individualities of those unlike us. I appreciate what college provided me. I made meaningful, lasting friendships and relationships. I was an athlete, so I was afforded the opportunity to travel and experience fine dining and lavish hotels while competing for the pride, honor, and integrity of the purple and white. I am a member of the first black Greek-lettered organization, which is Alpha Phi Alpha Fraternity Inc. At Wiley, we are Alpha Sigma Chapter 39, which is the first chapter west of the Mississippi River, allowing us the distinction of being heralded as a mother chapter. As a member of the fraternity, I embrace core principles and commonly refer to the aims of the organization, which are manly deeds, scholarship, and love for all mankind.

Affirm What You Know

Future king, I took a little time to share some of my story in this chapter to let you know that I have been where you are—not sure of my future, not sure of the path to take, and not sure if education was for me. Make no mistake about it, without an education, you put yourself at a disadvantage even before the race begins. When God blessed you with life, He equipped you with strength, power, and a natural curiosity to want to explore and interpret what you see and feel.

The scripture records in 2 Timothy 2:15, "Study to show thyself approved." What that means is that you have the ability to be the very best student and future leader possible, but it does require you to put work and effort into your academic studies and professional goals.

Your mind is open; it's up to you to fill it. The fact that you are reading this book tells me that you understand how important it is to enrich your life with different experiences and commentaries from those unfamiliar.

You have taken the time to strengthen your most valuable muscle—your mind. Don't crowd it with useless, futile, un-purposed doctrine or disrespectful undertones. Take a stance today to give your mind a workout every chance you can and, as we stated in the beginning of this chapter, strengthen it with things that will enhance it and make it stronger so you can support your future success with ideas of substance and merit.

EDUCATE YOURSELF TO FREEDOM

Your education is *yours*. No one can take it from you once you've acquired it, and the goal for you should be to acquire as much knowledge, insight, and information as you can absorb so that you are clear when you speak and rational when you listen.

In chapter 2, we spoke about the slave. The slave, though physically strong, was mentally weakened. The slave was not mentally weak; he was mentally weakened through abuse, atrocities, and depression.

To teach a slave to read or write was against the law. Slave owners and oppressors knew that once slaves received education, they would no longer be slaves, for an educated man is a free man.

Young prince, that is what I want to deposit into your spirit at this moment: stop being a slave! Educate yourself! Empower yourself! Redeem yourself! Free yourself! The choice is yours! College is mandatory—not an option. If you don't desire to go to a traditional four-year college, then better yourself by entering a community college or trade school. Keep your mind active. Don't allow yourself to become a slave, unaware.

I close the chapter with this: I was told a long time ago that if you ever want to keep information away from a black man, put it in a book! How many secrets have been kept from you?

5

THE POSTURE OF SUCCESS

Never look down on anybody unless you are helping them up.

—Rev. Jesse Jackson

Prince Artreal and
Prince Brandon

Well, sir, we have definitely spent some wonderful time together up to this point. My only desire is that you have learned from my experiences and stories thus far and understand how wonderful and important you are not only to this world but to yourself.

The value a man places on himself outweighs the criticism and opinions of others. You have to be determined to be the very best you can be. At the end of the day, all that matters is self-realization, self-actualization, self-worth, and self-esteem.

Your Majesty, you have to love yourself because in the end you're all you have. So many future kings have been devalued and torn down, losing sight of their unmerited power and uniqueness, lying dormant within. Hence, the reason for all the love and assuredness found in this book is to ensure that today's prince will become tomorrow's king!

SELF-VISUALIZATION

I take a lot of time to reiterate your titles. If you've noticed, I say things to you like *young man*, *prince*, *sir*, *future king*, and *Your Majesty* to complement more common terms like *my brother* and *young brother*. I do this for a reason: to erase years of being called things like *stupid*, *loser*, *failure*, *mistake*, *punk*, *liar*, *thief*, *fat*, *nigga*, and a host of other terms that degrade and demean you while tearing down your stance and self-esteem as a very proud, determined, confident young African American male and ultimately today's prince—tomorrow's king!

The way you see yourself may not be how the world sees you, but if the intent and purpose of this book accomplishes what it set out to do, truth be told, it won't matter how the world sees you. At the end of the day, it's all about how you see yourself; and though I can't see you physically, I know that if you are reading this, there is something magnificent and outstanding not only about your present, but your future as well, which is brighter than ever.

I'm proud of you. I'm proud of you for making the investment to increase your intellect while embracing a *you* that realizes you are a blessing, not a curse. You are strong, not weak. You are smart, not dumb. And though you are hated and hated on, you now know that the only thing that matters is that you love yourself and are going to treat others as you demand to be treated.

Make no mistake about it, you can't go around talking about living out your dreams while subjecting people to your nightmare. I have seen people attempt to dismantle a person's confidence by subjecting him or her to their own insecurities. I have seen people who are both small-minded and immature, trying to inflict their past hurts and pains on others without cause. I have watched cowards and bullies harass innocent, undeserving, and unsuspecting bystanders for the sheer joy of unleashing their own voids and depressions on someone less aggressive and less confrontational. Treat people with dignity, respect, and courtesy, and you will begin to see that what you give, you will receive. Your enemies and detractors may see you as nothing, but they will respect who you are and what you represent.

Future king, the purpose of this chapter is to posture you for success! The only way you can be successful is to have a clear understanding of your self-worth and make monumental investments in your own psyche and mental outlook so that, regardless of who or what attempts to derail you or take you off course, their efforts will fail because you are "postured for success."

As we take this journey together, rely on one thing: you have everything it takes to stand strong, be strong, live strong, and give strength to others, for that is what successful people do.

DEFINE SUCCESS

Working around so many young people, I often hear them hypothesize on or conjure an image or idea of what success is and resembles. I deem it necessary to first describe success in a manner applicable to your life.

Though I don't quote the dictionary often, *success* is defined as having a favorable or desired outcome, the attainment of wealth, favor, and eminence.

As you can see here, success is equated to achieving in some or every aspect of your life. Success is equated to having exorbitant amounts of money. Success is also equated to having superiority, prominence, and power. In essence, successful people are those who have reached the pinnacle of whatever endeavors they have tasked themselves to engage in.

PERCEIVED SUCCESS

The issue plaguing society today is that success has been associated with the accumulation of *things*. See, in theory, a successful person rides around in fancy cars, shops anywhere he desires, lives in a huge house with luxury bedrooms and bathrooms, and buys fancy jewelry and expensive objects just for the sake of saying he has them. The way society portrays success is all about how much you can get in this lifetime.

Future king, might I incline your attention to understand that success is so much more than what you can purchase and portray. Success is about fulfillment, benevolence, and accomplishment. It's about rendering assistance to your fellow brother or sister while also empowering them to strive and work toward their own level of success. It's about being able to reflect on your accomplishments and take pride in knowing you did it the right way. It was not necessary for you to step on others to be successful; rather, you assisted many along the way so that not only are you successful, but many others are successful alongside you. That, my brother, is what success is and how it should be portrayed. Success should be portrayed as having family and friends to share and make memories with. It should also suggest or imply that a successful person is a loved person. You can acquire all the things you desire in this world, but without love, things are fleeting and hold very little value—whereas you will remember a hug or a kiss from someone you love forever. It's time we start to embrace what's really important!

THE MIND FOR SUCCESS

Success is a mindset. A successful person may not have deep pockets, but a successful person is satisfied in knowing that he has a giving heart and loved ones to share experiences with. You see, a successful person understands the value of appreciating all life has to offer and finds solace in the accomplishments and prestige associated with being content and satisfied.

As I previously noted, success is a state of mind. To be successful, one has to posture himself to receive inspiration that will place him in a position to achieve his desired greatness. Before we really get into how to attain true success, it is imperative that we take a moment to analyze the fundamental aspects of success and ultimately where all success comes from.

THE TEST OF SUCCESS

I began my teaching career in 2000. I had recently moved to Houston, Texas, and started teaching at one of the well-known high schools in Sunnyside. The principal, Dr. Ronnie C. Evans Sr., embraced me and made me feel a part of the team and a part of his family. I appreciate Dr. Evans for believing in me when there wasn't much there. I was a science teacher, varsity-baseball head coach, and assistant band director. In my mind, I had it going on.

I had a fresh career, a fresh condo, and a fresh ride, and I was engaged to be married within two years' time. As I embarked upon my new career and newfound "success," I neglected to satisfy my responsibilities of acknowledging God's prominence in my life and respecting His influence toward all I was experiencing. I stopped working toward my goals of being a doctor and began stifling my growth due to arrogance, pride, and cockiness.

Future king, trust me when I tell you, God has a way of returning you to your rightful place and making you understand just how much He is needed in your life.

To teach in Texas, you have to be certified. Now, this may be the case in other states, but I can speak only about what I know. I needed to pass two qualifying exams to remain in my position as a teacher and coach. They gave me three years to accomplish this task. Because I was so arrogant and prideful and truly believed that the sun didn't rise until I got out of bed, I convinced myself that I had reached a level of success that could not be taken from me. I became complacent and nonchalant about the impending exams and took them for granted. I had no idea that this would be the thing that would turn me back to God.

I was reaching the end of my three-year grace period and decided that because I was such a good teacher, I would pass the exams, all would be fine, and I could continue being fabulous! Wrong! I failed. I took the test twice during the final year, and both times, I failed, forcing me to relinquish control of what I loved: my career, my money, my life! I became a substitute teacher in a place where I used to be an affecting, popular, and might I add, stylish teacher. I had fallen from grace because I was resting on false success.

To cut to the chase, I failed the teaching exam a total of seven times over the span of three years after I lost my position. Here I was, a college graduate with a master's degree, reduced to the position of a substitute teacher, a bus driver, a teacher's aide, a waiter at a strip club, and a nighttime associate at a major amusement park that is no longer operational. I lost money, power, influence, status, vehicles, friends, family, and I nearly lost my mind. It was a terrible place to be. I lost all hope and confidence in myself. I had failed—"but God!" (I'm sure you remember that from chapter 3.)

It was the morning of the first day of school in 2005. I was twenty-six years old and had been out of teaching for an entire year. I found myself in a deep depression based on my current reality. No job, no money, and very little faith. I had nowhere to go, nowhere to turn, and no one to help me out of the situation. Future king, when you find yourself in a situation or condition that has you confused, depressed, frustrated, or merely just looking for answers, don't look left. Don't look right. *Look up*! God sees and knows exactly where you are and what you need. Okay, back to that morning, while sitting on the bed, I prayed a simple open prayer to God. I said, "God, by the time I am thirty-five years old, if it be your will, I want to be a campus principal." Then I declared, "I am going to pass all necessary exams and have my own building by the age of thirty-five."

God had me right where He wanted me. I had nowhere else to turn except to Him. Here I was, the provider of my household, struggling month to month to keep the little piece of car we had in the driveway and scraping together just enough to keep the electricity and water on in a house that was in foreclosure every month, with no promise of payment or relief from debt. It was rough! We were classified as the working poor.

God had me in a position where I had to humble myself and begin to pray and talk to Him about my ego, character, and lack of humility. I had to repent and remember that He, and He alone, gets the glory for success.

I had given up on teaching until one night, I was speaking with a friend, and he told me, "You need to take the test again." There was an anointing behind his words because I felt like my time had arrived. Future king, God has a way of getting His message to us. That night, I knew God was conveying to me that I had suffered long enough and that the fulfillment of His promise to deliver me was at hand!

For anyone who knows me, I did what I do in every situation that requires a plan and execution: I called Cornelia. I told her that it was time for me to take the test again, and she said, "All right. I'll buy a book for you to study." Here I was, broke with no money, investing in myself. But God made provision and blessed her to be a blessing to me to aid me in my studies. Thank you, Cornelia, for always believing in me and being ready to assist at a moment's notice!

I studied every day and every night to the point of exhaustion. I was determined to succeed in passing my exams this time around. God granted me *favor*. He allowed me to succeed, and very quickly, all that I had lost was restored. I passed both exams and was certified to be a teacher.

I wasn't finished yet.

If you recall, a few paragraphs ago, I informed you that I prayed to be a principal by the time I was thirty-five. In 2008, I entered the principal's certification program, and during the summer of 2008, after one year of teaching, I was hired as an assistant principal at South Houston High School. During that time, I successfully completed the principal's program, and in 2009, I passed the principal's certification exam. I served as an assistant principal for five years. I encouraged students and gave God the glory all at the same time.

In August of 2013, at the age of thirty-four, with my thirty-fifth birthday merely three weeks away, God honored my prayer and request. I was called—not hired, but called—to be the principal at Jack Yates High School in Third Ward, Houston, Texas. God blessed me with all this because I believed, because I humbled myself, because I worked tirelessly toward my goals, and because I never doubted that God would do exactly what He said He would do.

And now, as a high school principal, I have reached a level of success I never imagined possible. But make no mistake about it, for all that I have accomplished, God now gets the glory. I am very careful to acknowledge Him in all I do and thank Him for all I receive. I have no doubt that because I appreciate and recognize Him in everything, abundance is on the horizon. As for me and my house, the best is yet to come—if you don't believe me, keep watching. I understand now that giving God what's due will usher you into your due and new season. A season of rest, peace, and prosperity! We should pause for a shout break because that's good news, and that news is applicable to you and your situation as well. Future king, let's come up and rise together—will you join me?

What am I saying to you? Life has a way of veering you off track in making you think that everything you've worked for is not going to happen. Because if that's the case, you have to continue to work toward your dreams and desires, and when the time is right, you won't have to find success; success will find you. Patience and determination make the difference in being tested in one moment and successful in the next. That's why it's imperative that you never quit because you may be right at the cusp—the precipice for change. And because of doubt and frustration, you quit right before the breakthrough! As stated in one of my favorite poems, "Don't Quit,"

> *Often the struggler has given up,*
> *When he might have captured the victor's cup,*
> *And he learned too late, when the night slipped down,*
> *How close he was to the golden crown.*
> *Success is failure turned inside out—*

The silver tint of the clouds of doubt,
And you never can tell how close you are—
It may be near when it seems afar;
So stick to the fight when you're hardest hit—
It's when things seem worst that you mustn't quit!"

—Author unknown

Future king, no matter what you do—never quit! You never know how close you are to making it.

For those of you who wrestle with why you can't attain the level of success you desire, I encourage you to keep fighting and keep pressing, for in due season, you will succeed if you don't quit. Romans 8:18 says, "For I reckon that the sufferings of this present time are not worthy to be compared with the glory which shall be revealed in you." Keep fighting, keep pressing, keep praying, and keep believing, for your best days, your glory days, and your successful days are still ahead of you.

SUCCESS IS DIVINE

According to the scriptures, Matthew 6:33 says, "Seek ye first the kingdom of God and His righteousness, and all these things shall be added unto you." Proverbs 3:6 goes on to add, "In all thy ways, acknowledge Him and He will direct your path." The concept being conveyed in both the New Testament and the Old Testament is that when we put our trust and confidence in God, then, and only then, will all the things we have set out to attain be provided to us because of our obedience, appreciation, and acknowledgment that God is our *Provider*.

Future king, if God is not the core of your aspiration and ambition, true success will be impossible to achieve. Now, notice I did not say success would be impossible to achieve, but rather, I noted that *true* success will be impossible to achieve. There are false senses of reality about what real success is and looks like. See, future king, a bank account with several zeros attached is not an indicator that true success has been gained. Oftentimes, you see individuals who have a significant amount of wealth, status, and popularity one day; but then, a few days later, they are broke, ostracized, and criticized for not being able to keep the status they once enjoyed. It's not to say that these people were irresponsible or did not have good business sense, but perhaps they missed the core principle that God had to be included in their plans if true success was their goal.

If you recall from the definition, the term *favor* was used to indicate success. Favor is something that comes from God. God is the only one who can grant favor. It basically means that doors are being opened for you in a manner that can't be explained. Young man, that's what God wants to do for you! You know you've worked hard, but once you hit the realm of "favor," things become very easy. It gets this way because you have continually acknowledged that God is the head of your life and because you have committed your works to Him. He is *required* to bless and sustain you.

As you learned in the last chapter, the only way you will reach this style of living is to stay in constant communication with God through prayer.

I have one more scripture to share with you to help you understand what it takes to reach true success. If you look at Proverbs 10:22, it states that "the blessing of the Lord makes rich, and He adds no sorrow with it." To translate that into today's vernacular, when God blesses you with success, riches, and favor, there is no strife in obtaining it and no grief and remorse in attaining it. In fact, not only will it be easy to attain, it will also be easy to maintain as long as you continue on the initial path where you appreciate and reverence God.

You can't forget to keep God in the plan. He is the originator of your success and will be the sustainer of it too as long as you continue to live according to His plan for your life.

A true blessing from God is not something you have to question or worry about. It will sustain you and your family. That's just how good God is. So before you say that you're successful or you want to be successful, check your motives and check your plan. Make sure God is involved from start to finish.

A SUCCESSFUL POSTURE AND STANCE

Okay, prince, now that we understand what is needed for success in regard to yielding control to God, let's figure out the posture of success. Successful people are inspirational in the face of tragedy and disaster. Successful people stand firm in their principles and convictions. Successful people are fearless and strong in the face of oppression and persecution but are also humble and meek when it comes to service and sacrifice.

A successful person walks with confidence and commits to his goals without hesitation and is unwavering. A successful person doesn't take days off or quit because it gets difficult and works tirelessly until the goal has been accomplished.

Young man, if you truly desire success, you have to understand up front that it comes with a price very few are willing to pay. Success comes with the burden very few are able to carry. Success comes with an attitude that says, "I will not quit until I'm complete. I will not stop until I'm finished. And I will not rest until I'm victorious."

The posture of success resembles a man who is not afraid to bow before his Heavenly Father as he seeks wisdom and guidance while standing firmly in the presence of his enemies to protect his family and friends. The posture of success is found in a man who will give himself to assist others while taking a stance to fight injustice in the face of oppression. The posture of success is found in a man who never looks down, for there is nothing on the ground but failure, regret, and shame. A successful man holds his head high with dignity and self-respect, with honor and loyalty, and with commitment and character.

The posture of success is found in a man who admits his wrongdoings and makes no effort to excuse his offenses. He owns his mistakes and defeats and renders the appropriate remarks or actions to suggest that he takes full responsibility for his actions.

Young man, I say to you that if you are to attain success, start walking like a man of success, start talking like a man of success, start exhibiting qualities of a man destined for success. Act as though success is in your grasp, speak as though success is on the tip of your tongue, and treat others as though you have already reached success and are now turning to assist them in being as successful as you have aspired to be.

The posture of success is one where you give rather than receive, bless rather than curse, love rather than hate, and work rather than rest!

Young man, in order for you to be successful, you have to take the first step, which is to put down the video game, turn off the television, set aside the cell phone, log off the Internet, let social media take care of itself, and activate your mind, body, and soul by committing to the dreams and desires you see for yourself. I guarantee that if you work toward any and every goal you've set for yourself, and you give it your very best effort, you will reach your goals. Retired linebacker Ray Lewis says is best: "The only thing that follows hard work is results."

Success, though a mindset, cannot be words alone. It requires you to inspire and motivate yourself. To be successful means you will encourage yourself when everyone else has written you off. Success means you will deny yourself fundamental needs and fundamental urges and desires so you may achieve ultimate greatness and superiority. To be successful means you will put effort, dedication, and determination into every endeavor you immerse yourself in. To be successful means you accept the fact that sometimes you may fail, but you are driven by the mindset that failure is not an option.

If that's you, you may be on the road to success!

SUCCESS IS ALL AROUND YOU

Future king, success has also taken on images. Society has portrayed success as being famous and having extreme status. I want you to understand that there are successful people all around you. The problem is that you don't recognize them. You see them but you don't honor their presence and influence in your life. In fact, the most successful people in your life are oftentimes taken for granted. For instance, your parents. They may not be the best people or the most responsible at times, but they are investing in you by spending time with you, clothing and feeding you, making sure you have some, if not all, of what you need, and doing their best to get you a percentage of what you want. That's a success story!

Every time a parent wakes you up for school and sends you out the door so you can receive an education, that's a success story! When a father works twelve to fourteen hours a day to make sure his family is fed and their needs are met, that's a success story!

Let's go a step further. Every day you go to school, and you're greeted by your principal, teacher, coach, bus driver, cafeteria worker, or some official for the sole purpose of making sure you are protected and educated—that's a success story.

Public educators are success stories. They went to college to obtain their degrees; some went on to earn masters and doctorate degrees. They sacrifice every day to provide you with knowledge, understanding, and expertise so you can have the life you desire. They are successful people because they have found fulfillment in influencing the lives of young people like you. Instead of students appreciating them, many students disrespect them and look down on them because they don't drive the fanciest vehicles or live in the best houses. Future king, if that's you, please stop! Educators need to be extolled for their sacrifices and appreciated for their contributions to your future success. Whether you have graduated from school or are still in school today, take time and appreciate those who are affecting your future daily!

Young brother, you have to change the way you view success. There are too many examples of success all around you. A single mother who can feed her children is a success! A young man who decides not to do drugs or sell them is a success! A young man who made the decision not to drive drunk, saving not only his life but the lives of others, is a success! A young man who graduates from high school, goes on to college, and graduates with his bachelor's degree and then decides to become a doctor and serve patients in his community is a success! A young man who gets caught up in the "heat" of passion and produces life, commits to being a real father and a real man, and makes his situation "blessed" by legitimizing his baby's mama, turning her into a wife, and being a provider and protector to his next generation is a success! The young man who decides to join the military to defend our rights and freedom is a success! The young man who decides to commit to a life of service by being a police officer or a firefighter, with the intent of keeping his neighborhood safe so children can play without the threat of being abused or taken, is a success!

There are success stories all around you. Don't be fooled into thinking you have to be on TV or you have to be rich to be successful. That's not success; that's a hustle. And like most hustles, eventually they get old, and the game is changed, leaving "hustlers" out of luck.

THE BLESSING TO BE SUCCESSFUL

And now, future king, I want to impart something to you. The fact that you are reading this book and understanding that you are surrounded with successful people makes you a success as well. I encourage you to change the way you see yourself and recognize that you are a success story as well. A successful person is a person who has failed but keeps trying. A successful person is a person who has messed up but doesn't give up on his dreams. A successful person understands that anything worth having is worth working for, worth sacrificing for, and worth fighting for.

Future king, when you want to see a successful person, there is no need to turn on the television set. I want you to find a mirror, look at yourself, and smile. Say out loud, "I am a success. I will be successful. God has blessed me to be a success, and I will work each day until I reach the level of optimal success."

Future king, success, like beauty, is in the eye of the beholder. Start speaking life into your situation. Start declaring and decreeing, "I have what I say I have and will become what I say I will become." And because I can, I decree over your life right now,

> You are great! You are noble and aristocratic! There is destiny inside you, and the promise of your life has not yet been fully revealed. You may have had it rough up to this point, but your success is at hand. It's time to start working toward the royalty associated with the rest of your life. Behold, *my* success is at hand!"

If you want to be a doctor, say to yourself, "I am a doctor!" Speak it into existence but understand that words without actions produce nothing. So start now in working toward becoming a doctor, which means making good grades in school, reading outside of your normal assignments, and spending time with doctors and health professionals by visiting and volunteering at the hospitals and finding internships and opportunities for exposure. You will be surprised how many people God will put in your life once you make your request known and start working toward it.

If you want to be a professional athlete, say to yourself, "I am a professional athlete!" Speak it into existence by faith and decree that you will play professional sports but understand that you have to train like a professional athlete, discipline yourself like a professional athlete, study like a professional athlete, eat like a professional athlete, and adopt the work ethic and dedication of a professional athlete. There is nothing that you cannot do if you commit to it.

Stop giving your dream lip service—give your dreams life!

6

HONOR AND INTEGRITY
(WORDS TO LIVE BY)

Where there is no shame…there is no honor.

—African proverb

Prince R.J.

I want you to know that I have thoroughly enjoyed and appreciated the opportunity to speak to you with such passion and sincerity. Young man, I believe in you! Though

I've never met you physically, because of the intimacy we've shared through written word and spiritual connection, I feel as though somewhere along the way, I will have the opportunity to shake your hand and applaud you for all you've gained and attained in realizing that you really are tomorrow's king.

It goes without saying that it is an awesome responsibility to be referred to as the heir to the throne, but allow me to alleviate your fears and calm your apprehensions. Young man, you are prepared! See, royalty is not something that can be wasted. It is something that must be embraced and processed. I refer to it as a process because it may take you a lifetime to reach your goals and uncover your true majestic potential, but when you do, you will then realize how amazing it is to be king.

Make no mistake about it, at this point, you don't have all the answers. Nor do you possess the wisdom required to enact substantial change not only in your life but in the lives of others. But because you are preparing yourself throughout the journey of this book, you are closer to tapping your untapped potential.

As I've already shared with you in previous chapters, I'm proud of you. You could be doing countless other things rather than reading a book aimed at shaping and molding your perceptions and realities into an image where you realize that life was not given to you by mistake but rather *on purpose*. Because you are purposed, the attacks are greater. Because you are purposed, the pain is more intense. Because you are purposed, your struggles will be tumultuous. But I say to you this day, because you are purposed, greater is your reward!

See, for all you've endured to get to this point—for all the frustration, ridicule, embarrassment, abandonment, pain, isolation, depression, abuse, neglect, and disappointment you've overcome—the inheritance that has been set aside for you once you've reached the point of wisdom and maturity will equip you to handle a blessing of such magnitude. You will then realize that for all you've been through, it was truly worth it.

But in order to be a king, you must embrace, recognize, and adhere to a standard of life. Words cannot be wasted on you. The experiences and conversations shared with you by seasoned adults will help shape your identity and add substance to your life. What point am I making? We, in this era, have lost the connection to our past, thereby hindering our advancement today. We no longer respect our history and deny the relevance of yesterday's fight in today's war.

I'm not going to reintroduce sections from previous chapters, but I wish to share with you two terms that still hold the same meaning as they did when our ancestors were not allowed to be classified as such. Because they were deemed as property, or chattel, they were not classified as humans but rather as possessions. To paint a better picture, our male ancestors were esteemed less than Caucasian women and were valued as three-fifths of a person, which is the equivalent of being 60 percent of a Caucasian man—just another history lesson so you will better understand the point I'm making.

Two terms should be associated with every man regardless of his age, race, or ethnicity. The two terms that I choose to introduce to you speak volumes of a man's self-worth and character. I am speaking of *honor* and *integrity*.

As the next few pages unfold, it is my sincere hope that once a better understanding has been established on what it means to have honor and integrity, you as a prince and future king will strive day in and day out to acquire titles of that magnitude. To be classified as honorable and with integrity is something to be sought after. Very rarely will you hear the terms separated. Ninety-nine percent of the time, if a man has honor, his best friend, integrity, lives on the same street, if not next door. You may feel like the words mean the same thing, but they have their own place and their own significance.

Let us begin!

WHAT IS HONOR?

Honor is a term used to distinguish noble individuals from those who don't understand the value of a name that has not been tarnished by a lack of commitment and empty or broken promises. The dictionary defines *honor* as being a concept that entails "a perceived quality of worthiness and respectability that affects both the social standing and the self-evaluation of an individual." *Honor* is also defined as "high stature based on actions and the embracing of a moral code."

An honorable man is one who acts in honesty, in fairness, and with a value of credit and distinction. A man who is honorable walks in the highest level of respect and has established himself to be a man classified with merit and accountability. An honorable man is one who is esteemed highly and exemplifies a walk of fame and glory. And while all this is true for a man with honor, what makes him deserving of the terms and distinctions mentioned above is that he is all these things in silence.

The reason I've chosen to indicate the voice of an honorable man as "silent" isn't because he can't speak or is not able to articulate himself. It is because for all that is said about him, it is never anything he speaks of about himself, but rather, it is observed in his conversation, his approach to dealing with situations, and his handling of people. To be honorable means you embrace the best parts of "man" while attempting to assist where there is a need. A man with high honor lends a helping hand instead of clenching his fist. To walk in honor means to walk with an erect posture with dignity, self-respect, and pride.

A man of honor understands the difference between arrogance and confidence and can navigate between the two with ease. He recognizes that arrogance is offensive and rude whereas confidence is reassuring and fortifying, a testament of preparedness and perseverance. To be honorable means to have respect not only for yourself but for all those around you. Future king, you have a responsibility to be the depiction of honor in everything you say and do. If your words don't match your actions, you need to check your conversation and work on the two reflecting each other. Words and deeds should resemble each other!

I know that to walk in the shoes of a prince is not an easy walk. You are often approached by some of the most deceitful, unscrupulous, shady people imaginable. As a result, it will cause you to be guarded and detached. It will cause you to take on the mentality of "I'll get you before you get me." And where I understand having to take that approach in a world where honor has been lost, I am encouraging you to find the decency in humanity again. I am encouraging you to seek out individuals who walk in the truest form of morality and uprightness and embrace their stance and position as they address the "human condition" and the need for change. The time is nigh for you to drop the "trust no one" and "get over on everyone" mentality, for that is not an honorable approach in addressing a cancerous condition.

A man of honor possesses an inner strength uncommon in most. A man of honor has a level of restraint and temperament that all should strive to emulate. A man of honor is slow to speak and quick to listen. A man of honor does not judge a situation speedily but instead uses concrete evidence and discernment as he attempts to find the truest course of rectitude.

An honorable man has an honorable family. A man of honor embraces his wife as an honorable woman. An honorable man doesn't have a family of shame. He ensures that his wife and children understand their value and makes sure they are his priority.

A man of honor works tirelessly. He sometimes has to secure two or even three jobs to make sure his family has the best this world has to offer. He teaches through example and partnership while making sure he does not sink below his convictions and established standards.

Future king, you, as an up-and-coming man, should aspire to walk in this manner. For the validity of your kingdom, I encourage you to embrace principles of honor and understand that, in this world, you have only one thing that belongs to you outright. It's not your possessions; it's your name. When you are referred to or your name is called, it should signify accomplishment, respect, decency, and honor. For a man without these virtues attached to his existence needs to analyze his intentions and rectify his reputation. Honor is something you work a lifetime to gain but can lose in a second. Make sure your motives are pure and your right hand knows what your left hand is doing at all times. You have a natural proclivity to do what's right and live an honorable life. Despise the shame and do it. The choice is yours!

What Is Integrity?

Wow! Who knew there is so much to be associated with honor? And if you recall, during the opening section of this chapter, I told you that honor and integrity live next door to each other; and if they don't, they live on the same street. Well, because *honor* is such a powerful term, without it, it is very difficult to have integrity. Integrity, like honor, is a term and distinction every prince and future king should embrace.

Integrity is a powerful way to classify or describe a man. By definition, *integrity* is the acknowledgment and acceptance of moral and ethical principles. To have integrity, one must be honest, unimpaired, and unbiased. A man with integrity has a state of being that is whole and complete. He is a man with character, honor, and pride.

Now, let's talk about pride for second. Pride is one of those terms that, if used in the incorrect context, takes on an undesirable connotation. Pride has been associated with arrogance and stubbornness. It is a condition that befalls us all, and we have to work diligently toward lowering pride and raising the levels of humility in our lives. Being humble and meek affords us the opportunity to learn and be fulfilled with what is appropriate and blessed. If you recall from the scriptures, "The meek shall inherit the earth; and shall delight themselves in the abundance of peace!" (Ps. 37:11).

As a man, it is important that you embrace the principles of being humble. Humility and weakness are not the same thing. Weakness is a sign of defeat whereas humility is a sign of unwavering strength and the confidence of knowing that you are assured a breakthrough as long as you are patient. I know we are talking about integrity, but I felt the need to add that.

Okay, now that we are focused again, let us continue.

For a man with integrity, pride suggests that he is not above working hard for what he believes in. He is oftentimes solid in his stance on not receiving special treatment, handouts, or unmerited assistance. Pride, in relationship to integrity, should be applauded and not discouraged.

I wanted to make sure that the two connotations of pride were not misrepresented as I attempt to define integrity. Perhaps, the term *proud* should replace *pride* because a proud person is one who earns everything he possesses. A proud person appreciates his accomplishments and renders service to others in need without the desire of compensation and open recognition.

It's funny that, back in the day, to appreciate a man for his contributions to your project or solicited need (i.e., painting a house, moving, or fixing a car), a six-pack, a box of chicken, the assuredness that the favor will be reciprocated, and a handshake were enough to say how much the support was appreciated. Nowadays, because people operate in such dishonor and lack of integrity, with impure motives tainted with the desire to be paid or hooked up, their assistance is usually camouflaged in some effort to gain rather than give.

That's not the way life was intended. We were put here to assist one another and to do it with a pure heart and with selfless motivation.

A man of integrity does all he can to protect his family and friends from degradation and shame. An integrity-driven man makes sure his motives and intentions are pure and his affairs are above reproach. He makes sure the appearance of evil is diminished because of his reputation and his record of honesty and high moral character.

Young man, strive to operate in integrity. Integrity is synonymous with reputation. If your integrity is shattered because of selfishness, ego, or need, you may not be able to repair the damage. Proverbs 22:1 says, "A good name is more desirable than great riches; to be esteemed is better than silver or gold." Future king, always fight to keep a clear name. Its value supersedes riches and glory. Its value is everlasting. There are people today whom you remember because of the legacy they left behind. Because you are great and will contribute significantly toward the advancements of tomorrow, work diligently in making sure that your name is spoken by lips of appreciation and admiration, not disrespect and ridicule. You are, and deserve, better than that.

But young man, I don't want you to get caught up in man's perception of you in this section. Integrity is more about how you perceive yourself and your actions. Integrity inevitably deals with intrinsic convictions and moral awareness. The question is, how do you see yourself?

See, a man with integrity recognizes that it is most important to be able to look in the mirror and know that he is living a life that is acceptable and pleasing not only to himself but to God. A man of integrity takes the necessary steps to examine himself thoroughly with a very critical eye. A clear conscience always renders a good night's sleep.

Future king, it's not difficult to deceive a person, but you can't deceive yourself and God. It's not difficult to persuade a person to try and sell drugs, especially when you flash the right amount of cash, but you know that you lead a person down the wrong path, and there is no honor or integrity in that. It's not difficult to hustle or con an unsuspecting, naive person, but it is a shameful event for you to know that you took advantage of someone.

My point is simple: You can fool some of the people some of the time. You can fool all the people all the time. But you can't fool God, and you can't fool yourself.

When a man operates in integrity, his only desire is to walk as an example of sophistication, education, glorification, and sanctification. A man of integrity has the mindset to keep his name and his reputation clear and free from scrutiny and judgment. A man of royalty such as yourself should want to embody integrity with every word, action, or deed.

Incorporate integrity into every facet of your life and dealings, and I guarantee that you will be perceived as a man walking in the office of honor with impeccable integrity.

DESPISING THE SHAME

I know this is not part of the title, but *shame* is another term that needs to be examined while I have your attention. Young man, I'm not going to quote the dictionary for this section, but I am going to give you my perception of how shame is running wild in the world today. African American males are unaware and oblivious of how they are perceived. It's not because they don't hear it from their elders; it's that they don't care what anyone thinks about how they look, dress, or feel. It's fearful how deep the roots of shame have been embedded into our psyche.

Young man, you have a responsibility to educate your brothers and sisters about how they are perceived in the eyes of their peers and contemporaries. It's not about worrying how others are viewing you or judging you; it's more about having self-respect and pride in your race and culture. I know that we have reached a period in time where it's okay to express yourself and "do you," but there has to be a point where we recognize just how *unrecognizable* we are nowadays.

There used to be a time when men dressed as men and carried themselves as men with honor and integrity, but today, we are dressing in ways that make a person pause and say, "Hmm?" Guys, please, let's put away the skinny jeans, unless that's truly your size, and reserve the capris for the ladies. Trust me, women look better wearing them than we will any day!

If you recall from chapter 2, you as a prince and future king were classified as being noble. I went on to share just how aristocratic you are. Young men who carry those titles carry themselves very well. They dress with a certain level of sophistication, style, and grace not common to most. They speak with eloquence and articulate themselves with conviction, focus, and clarity in complete sentences. They address people with the sincerity and reverence they deserve.

They respect women. They respect women. they respect women! Yes, I know I said it three times and capitalized with the progression of the statements, but, future king, we must do a better job in this area. We are disrespecting the one person that God made just for us, our women! God didn't create for us hoes, sluts, tramps, tricks, and bitches! He blessed us with queens, princesses, ladies, girlfriends, and ultimately wives or *helpmates*!

I can hear you now saying, "Well, they don't act like girlfriends or wives. They act like bitches and hoes so that's how I treat them." To that, I say to you, future king, it is your responsibility to love them *out* of that mentality and help them understand that there is a better way to get your attention, and let it be known that you are looking for quality. What woman doesn't want quality? And for that matter, what man doesn't deserve a quality woman?

You deserve the very best. Stop settling for less, but also, stop disrespecting those who don't know they are more—instead, help them!

Shame is an ugly way to be seen. It means you have very little awareness of how you are perceived and viewed against others like you in similar situations.

Future king, it's time we represent ourselves better. Let's pull up our pants and stop saggin'. Leave something for the imagination and stop exposing yourself to the world. All that you're showing belongs to your future wife. Stop showing off and giving away your best parts. I think I'm going to high-five myself on that one! Besides, when you look at it more closely, saggin' spelled backwards reads *niggas*, and you know how we feel about using and being associated with that term. Make a change in your appearance and present yourself as the king you're growing into!

Future king, please stop covering your body in so much ink. Your skin is beautiful, and the color is sought after by every race, culture, and ethnicity. Why do you think so many people tan themselves? To look like you! Unfortunately, once you put all the ink on your skin, we can't tell what you look like anymore, and it is nearly impossible for you to get a job with a substantial financial attachment. And please don't be fooled by what you see from athletes and entertainers. Make no mistake about it, I love sports and all they represent. I appreciate struggle and teamwork and admire the tenacity and dedication it takes to make it to the top, but, prince, that reality only exists for a select few. That only works in their world. I have never seen a banker, doctor, lawyer, teacher, police officer, or accountant with tattoos everywhere. Wake up, young brother, everything that glitters *isn't* gold!

Future king, let's do more reading and writing. I am proud of you for reading this book, but you have to keep reading so you can make quality statements and increase your vocabulary.

Future king, let's embrace the concept of family and stop abandoning our children to be raised by women. It took two to make the baby, and, truth be told, it takes two to raise it. If you have fathered a child, make sure you are there playing an active role in the life of that child. During slavery, they separated us on purpose to keep us weak and depressed. Now we are doing the same thing to ourselves—on purpose.

We have to stop the cycle and recognize what we are doing to ourselves. We are bringing shame to ourselves. Now is the time to stop! We have to make more of an effort to uplift and motivate our people. In the end, "we all we got!"

7

THE CHALLENGE, YOUR LEGACY

It took a lot of blood, sweat, and tears to get to where we are today, but we have just begun. Today we begin in earnest the work of making sure that the world we leave our children is just a little bit better than the one we inhabit today.

—President Barack H. Obama

Prince Rudy

Prince, we have reached the end of our journey together. The funny part about us being at the end is that, in essence, this is actually the beginning. Over the past six chapters, we've had the opportunity to laugh, smile, cry, share, pray, express, declare, decree, and forgive. You and I have spent valuable time affirming our faith and expressing a fundamental need for God in our lives.

We've walked through the scriptures. We've looked back into our past while simultaneously looking forward into the future to see just how much we can learn from yesterday as we make a conscious effort to contribute significant investments toward tomorrow.

I pray that you have enjoyed heightening your sense of awareness and responsibility in regard to your becoming a more formidable, confident man in today's society.

Future king, rest assured that making adjustments in your own life will better not only you but also your family and surrounding community. There is so much promise inside you. The impact you are going to make in this world will be tremendous. Such is the case because you understand your significance, your worthiness, and your responsibility to usher in a sense of belonging and purpose amid your people.

As you go forward in life, recognize that there will be those who want nothing more than for you to fail, but that's when you take inventory of your character within and recognize that all you have, all you've gained, and all you've survived through are a reminder and a testament that you have earned everything you've received. Because you've earned it, it entitles you to sit at the head of the table, for that is where you, as a king, belong.

In this, our final moments together, I will attempt to send you out with a king's decree and a king's blessing.

Thank you for taking the time to enrich your life by reading the words that I feel in my heart God has blessed me to share with you. Though I don't know you, I love you!

Be encouraged and of good faith and confidence that "greater is He that is in You, than he that is in the world" (1 John 4:4).

THE KING'S DECREE

If you look in the book of Exodus and start reading in the second chapter, you will find the story of a little baby who was placed in a bassinet to be sent up the river that he might have a chance to survive. During this time, the Egyptian king was murdering Hebrew babies as the population was growing too rapidly, and there was concern that the Hebrews might revolt and subdue the Egyptians.

This baby had purpose. This baby had promise. This baby had an incredible assignment that only he could fulfill.

Future king, though I'm not finished telling the story of this baby, I want you to know that it does not matter the situation you were born in or what is going on around you now, when your life is purposed and you've been called by God to complete an assignment, there is nothing in this world that will prevent God from using you and getting the glory from your life.

Though it might be difficult, you have to stop looking around and making excuses about where you come from, where you've been, what you've seen, what you didn't have, or who walked out and didn't support you. Because God has anointed you, He will get His use out of you.

What a blessing it is to know that I can't stop the promise of God in my life.

Back to the story. So here you have a Hebrew baby, born to his Hebrew mother, endowed with Hebrew blood, and because of his birth, was born a slave.

The Hebrew people during this time were in bondage. They were subjected, like our ancestors, to intense working conditions, intense brutality, intense pain and frustration. They were both oppressed and depressed, continually looking for salvation and freedom from such contemptuous conditions.

This mother wanted more for her Hebrew baby. From his birth, she made the choice to give him every opportunity to survive and to be more than she or her people were. She sacrificed that he might have a chance to experience the best this world had to offer.

Please allow me to thank all the mothers who have sacrificed so much for their children.

So again, the baby was sent up the river and was found by the daughter of the Egyptian king, better known as Pharaoh. Pharaoh's daughter took one look at the baby and immediately fell in love with him. She made the decision to keep him. In her words, "this baby is a blessing from the gods."

Future king, God has a way of taking care of His own. Though this baby should have grown up to build pyramids, he was instead taught to embrace Egyptian customs and traditions. He was educated by the Egyptians and groomed to support and administer Egyptian doctrine. But there was something unique about this baby; he was Hebrew and was destined to avenge the wrongs perpetrated against his people.

Moses is whom we are speaking of. Moses was born without the riches and glory associated with being Egyptian. But because of the call on his life, God saw fit to have him embraced by his enemy. Moses was raised and educated inside the very structure he was destined to destroy.

Moses, a Hebrew, was treated as an Egyptian, respected as an Egyptian, and revered as an Egyptian; but in the contrary, Moses could not relate to the Egyptians. There was something about Moses that caused him to struggle, in my opinion, from within.

Because he had a different type of blood flowing through his veins, there was always something drawing him back to his own people.

Now, let's go a little deeper into the story.

There was a taskmaster beating a Hebrew slave. Moses, being Egyptian by naturalization, was allowed to walk among his people as if he were not one of them; but as he observed the abuse, the blood—that's right, the blood—inside Moses began to be agitated. As a result of his blood being stirred from within, a conflict emerged between who he believed he was on the outside versus who God called him to be on the inside.

That conflict caused Moses to take action against the Egyptian. Moses had reached a point where he could no longer live in duality and continue to participate in the relentless atrocities committed against his people.

Moses killed that Egyptian for trying to take the dignity and strength from his Hebrew brother, though unknown. The part of Moses that embraced being Egyptian was being overtaken by what he was born to be, the redeemer of the Hebrew people!

Moses fled his home, his family, his friends, his traditions, and everything he knew. God drove him from that place so He could inform him of his purpose and mission.

Future king, such is the case with you. Oftentimes, God has to separate you from what you know so that He can give you what you need. As you've gone through the journey of this book, you've separated yourself from everything you've known and everything you've heard so that God can position you to identify your promise, destiny, and anointing.

So as Moses was driven from Egypt, God guided Moses through life with the understanding that there was something special about him and that there was still work for him to do.

Some forty years had passed at this point, and then, all of a sudden, God spoke to Moses directly. God took on the form of consuming fire and embodied the presence of a bush.

Though the bush was on fire and because He is also a keeper and preserver, it never burned.

The purpose was that with Him being Almighty God, He could've used anything He wanted to deliver His message, but He chose to use the one He anointed before his birth. He chose to use the one that He sent up the river to be raised and educated by those He was preparing to judge. God chose Moses just as God is choosing you.

Moses was told that he would be the deliverer of his people and, future king, by faith, I believe that you are chosen to be the deliverer of your people. Moses gave several excuses and reasons why he could not do what God required him to do, but once God has chosen you, there is no abandoning the mission.

God gave Moses simple commandments. In time, Moses returned to Egypt to perform God's wonders. Though he was not received in the beginning, Moses was not deterred from performing God's will and carrying out his assignment. This was Moses's life work, and he was called to see it through.

God got the glory out of Moses, and Moses fulfilled his agenda, which was to free the Hebrews, God's chosen people, and lead them out of bondage with the hope of a better life.

Overcoming Yourself

Future king, I took the time to go through the bullets of that story to encourage you in knowing that God has already chosen you. He has already purposed your life. He has decided where and how you will influence this world. All you have to do is listen for His voice and follow His plan.

Like Moses, sometimes God has to remove us from a situation and put us in a position that will provoke us to change. Moses encountered an internal conflict that prompted change.

On one hand, he was raised to be an Egyptian, but on the other hand, he was filled with Hebrew blood. Inside were pieces of him that wanted to serve many gods as the Egyptians were polytheistic, but because he was Hebrew, he did battle with the blood inside him that said there is but one God. Hebrews are monotheistic, which means they worship and serve the One God.

The Egyptian pieces of him rationalized and justified the notion that it was okay to hold another race of people down to accomplish futile missions such as building monuments and pyramids while the Hebrew parts of him resounded in his heart and viewed the treatment of his people as wrong. He was reminded, "I am my brother's keeper and together we will rise."

Future king, you very well may be the Moses for your family, the Moses for your community, and the Moses for this generation.

Separate yourself from what is not like you. You can't live your life as others have made you think is acceptable when you know inside that God is requiring more from you.

You have to elevate yourself, extract yourself, and recognize that the honor bestowed upon you is not common to most. No one on this planet can make the difference you can make. No one on this planet can run your race like you can run it. No one on this planet can be you better than you can be you, so, future king, recognize that God has anointed you to persevere and progress, to struggle and survive, and to redeem and resolve the hurts, pains, and frustrations that have plagued the generations before you and the current situation you find yourself in now.

You have the authority to change your situation and the situations of those around you. You have that power! You have been taught that you can speak and free yourself. You have been taught that you can speak and free your family. You have been taught that you can speak, and your situation will take on a new identity.

I challenge you to be better than you were yesterday. I challenge you to live above and not beneath. I challenge you to not only fly, future king, but to soar and reach the heights of your truest potential.

I challenge you to leave a legacy for your future generations of perseverance, commitment, sacrifice, education, wealth, and love.

Love is the great equalizer. Love is the greatest gift anyone can receive. Love will carry you when finances are not available. Love will heal the brokenhearted. Love will restore your faith in humanity and family and friends who have disappointed you.

God is love, and the gift from God to us is love that will never fail, die, or forget. If you remember from chapter 3, "For God so loved the world that He gave." What did He give? He gave love in the form of His Son, Jesus.

He loved us so much that He denied Himself His Son that you and I might have continual access to Him, and He with us.

It is now your time, Your Majesty, to pick up your crown and sit on your throne, a throne that has been glazed with grace and mercy, a throne that has been fortified with forgiveness and fulfillment, a throne that has been imbued and infused with sacrifice and love. Though the head of the one who wears the crown is heavy, it comes with the satisfaction of knowing that you are to lead a passionate group of people because of your maturity, insight, and wisdom. You have earned everything you've acquired, and as you lead, never forget that your crown and throne were made just for you!

THE KING'S BLESSING

Your Majesty, I say this through the blood under the anointing of God the Father: Go in peace. May the Lord bless you and keep you. May the Lord make His face shine upon you and be gracious unto you. May the Lord lift His countenance upon you and give you peace. May the Lord bless you to be the head and not the tail. May the Lord bless you to be above and never beneath. May the Lord bless you to be the lender and not the borrower. May the Lord bless you as you go out and come in. May the Lord bless you in the cities and in the fields. May the Lord bless you with houses that you did not build and vineyards you did not plant. May the Lord keep you in perpetual remembrance that you are loved and deemed greater and not the least. May the Lord bless your children and future generations to experience life more abundantly. May the Lord bless you with long life, health, and prosperity. May the Lord keep you now, henceforth, and forevermore. In Jesus's name, I declare and decree—*long love the king*!

ABOUT THE AUTHOR

Donetrus G. Hill is a high school principal, father, student advocate, speaker, and mentor. He is a graduate of Wiley College in Marshall, Texas, and is a current doctoral student earning his doctorate in educational leadership and management. He is a native of Saginaw, Michigan, and became a resident of Shreveport, Louisiana. Upon completing college, he moved to Houston, Texas, where he currently resides. Donetrus is passionate about the advancement and progression of African Americans and more specifically, the education and spiritual knowledge of males. He is committed to addressing the deficits and voids associated with their existence and affirming their position in society as formidable, capable individuals with much to contribute to society as a whole. Donetrus has been quoted as saying, "I am just a simple man who sees a great need."